THE CELTIC JERSEY

Published by Vision Sports Publishing in 2022

Vision Sports Publishing Ltd
19-23 High Street
Kingston upon Thames
Surrey
KT1 1LL
www.visionsp.co.uk

ISBN: 978–1913412–43–2

Editor: Jim Drewett
Editorial production: Ed Davis
Art director: Doug Cheeseman
Historical shirt consultant: Simon Shakeshaft
Reprographics: Jörn Kröger and Bill Greenwood
Print production: Ulrika Drewett
Commercial director: Toby Trotman

Photos: Getty Images, SNS, Shutterstock, Colorsport,
Alamy, PA Photos, Offside, Mirrorpix, Topfoto

Printed and bound in Slovakia by Neografia

A CIP Catalogue record for this book is available from the British Library

ABOUT THE AUTHOR

Paul John Dykes is the author of the following books:

The Quality Street Gang (2013)
Celtic's Smiler: The Neilly Mochan Story (2015)
Hoops, Stars & Stripes: The Andy Lynch Story (2016)
The Celtic Jersey (2022)

He was also the executive producer of the feature-length
documentary, *Celtic's Smiler: The Neilly Mochan Story* (2015)

Paul John's podcast, *A Celtic State of Mind*, has won
multiple awards and can be found on iTunes,
YouTube, Spreaker, Acast, and many other podcast players.

Paul John can be contacted on Twitter @PaulJohnDykes.

THE CELTIC JERSEY

THE COMPLETE HISTORY OF THE WORLD-FAMOUS HOOPS

By PAUL JOHN DYKES

CONTENTS

FOREWORD

By Tom Boyd, Celtic FC Ambassador

Tom Boyd lifts the League Cup in 2000

For me, the iconic green and white hoops of Celtic Football Club represent pride, passion and success.

When I see the famous jersey, it always takes me back to my childhood and the first time I was taken to Celtic Park by my father for my initiation into 'The Celtic Way'. I vividly recall standing in the 'Jungle' all those years ago, gazing out from the terracing and seeing those beaming green and white strips. They looked so clean and bright to my youthful eyes and it was always a dream of mine to one day pull on that jersey for real.

That day finally came on 8th February 1992 when I made my Celtic debut against Airdrieonians in a 2-0 league win. It was a real honour and thrill to wear the famous jersey for the first time, but I do recall that the home shirt was not without its critics that season. Celtic's shirt sponsors were Peoples Ford, whose logo was red, white and blue. It seems very strange now, and certainly caused some controversy at the time, that Celtic allowed the colours of their greatest rivals to appear on the hoops. I'm sure it wouldn't happen today.

When I joined Celtic, club legend Neilly Mochan was the kitman. All the kitmen I came across in my football career were the

same when it came to trying to get kit off them – it was as if the cost of them was coming out of their own personal pockets; they were so tight! Every item of kit that Neilly had was a prisoner; it was even a struggle to get a new pair of socks off him. But he was a great guy who had a brilliant sense of humour.

It is important for the players, as well as the fans, to have a stylish strip. I always wanted the kits to be a good fit, have a comfortable feel, and I never wanted the hoops to be over-complicated. The away strip was a different matter entirely, and we had – in my personal opinion – some terrible change kits when I was playing! Luckily most of Celtic's biggest triumphs have come wearing their traditional hoops.

The simplicity of the green and white hoops are quintessentially Celtic and they are recognised the world over. I remember we even used to wear them against Hibernian, despite the fact that they wore green and white jerseys too. Back in 2001, both Celtic and Hibs wore their away jerseys in the Scottish Cup Final. After we'd won the game 3-0, we changed from our yellow jerseys into the hoops to lift the cup and for the photographs that would go into the history books.

It was different a few years earlier, when we clinched the league title on the last day of the season at Celtic Park on 9th May 1998. That was a hugely emotional day because it was the first time we had won the league in 10 years and we stopped Rangers winning a 10th title in a row. All the players were caught up in the euphoria of the occasion,

so we didn't question it when we were asked to change into Umbro t-shirts for the presentation of the league trophy. When I look back at the photos now, I always regret that we weren't wearing the hoops.

I am sure that I speak for all Celtic fans when I say that the hoops should never be changed, but I also feel that Celtic should never have numbers on the backs of their jerseys. There was always an added individuality and uniqueness to Celtic when we had the numbers on the shorts instead. The club crest and manufacturer logo had been introduced over the years, but having numbers on the back of the hoops just didn't look right when they were worn in European matches after 1975. The matter was eventually taken out of Celtic's hands in 1994 when they were forced to introduce a numbering system on the shirts for domestic games.

It's incredible to think how much the history of this great club is intertwined with its kit. Nearly every variation of the shirt, home and away, is featured on the 300 or so pages of *The Celtic Jersey*. It is a simply wonderful book and a fantastic way to look back at the history of our famous club. I hope you enjoy it as much as I have.

C'mon The Hoops!

> "It was a real honour and thrill to wear that famous jersey for the first time"

MORE THAN JUST A SHIRT

An extraordinary club founded in extraordinary circumstances, Celtic Football Club's world-renowned jersey is arguably the most iconic shirt in the game

Celtic FC is no ordinary football club, and its famous green-and-white-hooped shirts are a globally recognised symbol of everything that it stands for.

The roots of the club's existence can be traced back to Ireland's Great Hunger (*An Gorta Mór*) in the mid-1800s, during and after which thousands of impoverished immigrants fled across the Irish Sea to Glasgow. Unlike those who made it to America, the Irish immigrants who made their home in Scotland did not see a drastic improvement in their quality of life.

Dismayed by the continued poverty of Glasgow's Irish immigrant population and inspired by Edinburgh's Hibernian Football Club, Andrew Kerins – known by his religious name of Brother Walfrid – decided to establish a football team to raise money for the 'penny dinner' scheme he had already set up to feed the city's "needy children". The club's primary objective would not be to win trophies but "to supply the east end conferences of the St Vincent de Paul Society with funds for the maintenance of the dinner tables of our needy children in

"The famous hoops not only represent the club's Irish roots, they epitomise the spirit of football for the greater good of a community"

Celtic captain Billy McNeill carrying the League Cup after the 2-1 victory over Rangers in 1965. Also in the picture are Neilly Mochan (far left) and John Clark (to Mochan's right) – two of Celtic's iconic kitmen the missions of St Mary's, Sacred Heart and St Michael's."

Beyond that immediate need, as Celtic's modern social mission statement states, Brother Walfrid also "saw the need for social integration and his vision was a football club that Scottish and Irish, Protestants and Catholics alike could support. A new football club would be a vehicle to bring communities together... The Marist brother sought for the club to have both a Scottish and Irish identity, hence the club's name 'Celtic' came about, representing a bridge of cultures across the Irish Sea... Celtic Football Club is a Scottish football club with proud Irish links... It is run on a professional business basis with no political agenda... The club always has been and always will simply aim to be the team of the people."

The famous hoops, therefore, not only represent the club's Irish roots, they epitomise the spirit of football for the

The Celtic dressing room pictured in 1967, the heyday of the hoops

greater good of a community. Or, as the late, great Tommy Burns, who was raised in the Calton area of Glasgow, put it: "When you pull on that jersey, you're not just playing for a football team... you're playing for a people and a cause."

Over the course of its history, however, the hoops have also come to represent something more. With success on the pitch and a style of play that has lifted its supporters to heights of emotion that its founding father could never have envisaged, the jersey has come to symbolise a tradition of triumph, with trophies won in an enchanting, swashbuckling manner.

As Jock Stein – the manager who masterminded the first British victory in the European Cup in 1967, with a team of players famously all born within 30 miles of Celtic Park – put it: "Celtic jerseys are not for second best, they don't shrink to fit inferior players."

The mystical allure of the green and white hoops has enchanted both football fans and players for generations. When Celtic were interested in signing former Newcastle striker Eddie Connelly in the early 1940s, it emerged that a Celtic jersey that he had been gifted by Willie Maley in 1937 had been worn under his own team's shirt during every game he had played ever since.

In 2008, Paolo Di Canio claimed that he had aspirations to play for Celtic after taking a shine to their jersey when playing Subbuteo as a child in Rome.

"There was a squad with horizontal green and white lines," explained Di Canio. "I was captivated by the colours of the shirt.

Despite the addition of sponsor logos, the hoops have maintained their iconic allure – not least the centenary kit as worn here by Pat Bonner, Peter Grant, Mark McGhee and Tommy Burns following the 1989 Scottish FA Cup triumph

kitman Neilly Mochan had packed a spare set of hoops in the kit hamper and the Rosenberg players did get their mementos, with one player commenting, "This is the strip all the world recognises as Celtic's."

Perhaps the allure of the hoops is best summed up in Kevin Graham's 2018 poem, *The Celtic Jersey*:

Iconic is a status that is earned and
achieved,
But ours was bonded when born, woven
and weaved.
In the hill mills by the diaspora of the
founding fathers,
To be loved by those that will hold it dear.

A whispered 'hello', a remembered goodbye,
A reflection of the fabric of history always
on the eye.
Even as time sees the film fade,
The textures turn, the colours change
shade.
The feeling remains the same.

A vision of against-the-odds success,
A testament to the sweat and skill
Of those whose souls are now stitched in
the material,
Binding it together.
Always beating hearts beneath the badge.

The jersey never shrunk to fit inferior
players,
And it will never weigh heavy on the
shoulders,
Of those with the strength to wear it,
And the will to believe in it.

I decided if one day I became a footballer I would like to play in Scotland. After 10 years playing in Italy, an offer came from Glasgow and I decided straight away to go to Celtic because my dreams would come true. The first time I wore the Celtic shirt was emotional for me. I was like a child who has just received a big present."

The Celtic jersey has a global appeal that few football shirts can match. When Jock Stein's team travelled to Norway in 1972 to wrap up a 5-2 aggregate victory against Rosenberg in the first round of the European Cup, the Scandinavians wanted to swap shirts after the match. However, Celtic were wearing their all-green away kit for the game and the home players refused to accept these less-celebrated jerseys. Thankfully,

"The Celtic jersey has a global appeal that few football shirts can match"

CHAPTER ONE
THE EARLY YEARS

1888-1936

ORIGINS OF THE HOOPS

Although it has always been green and white, several different versions of the Celtic home jersey were worn before it evolved into the famous hoops

In the early days of football, when clubs were being formed all over Britain, the choice of playing colours was often decided on a whim or based on practical or economic considerations like what shirts players already possessed or the cheapest jersey available. Indeed, the fledgling clubs which survived these pioneering days often changed colours on numerous occasions. For Celtic, like the many other clubs that had emerged in Scotland from Irish roots, green was the inevitable choice of primary colour. But the story of how this evolved into the famous green and white hoops we know today is a less logical – and in some ways fortuitous – tale.

Celtic's early history was interwoven with that of Hibernian FC, who had been formed in 1875. After the Edinburgh men won the Scottish Cup in 1887 (wearing green-and-white-hooped shirts with 'HFC' monogrammed on the front), their entire official party – including the committee, players and trainers – were entertained at St Mary's Parish Hall in the Calton area of Glasgow, and among the hosts were several of the men who were to serve on Celtic's first committee. They listened with considerable interest when Hibernian's secretary, in response to one of several toasts,

spoke and ended his oration with these fateful words: "Why don't you in the west of Scotland do as we have done in the east?"

Within a few months Celtic FC was founded, ironically recruiting several players from Hibernian. With these clear connections it is understandable that historians have suggested that the original Hibernian strip was the inspiration for the famous Celtic hoops. However, this is not the case and in fact the very first Celtic jersey was white.

When the first Celtic side (a collection of players recruited from other clubs) trooped out from their primitive pavilion on the evening of Monday, 28th May 1888 to play against Rangers Swifts, each player (the goalkeeper included) wore a white woollen shirt, topped with a green laced-up collar. The first Celtic crest (a green celtic cross within a red oval) was positioned on the right breast. The shorts (or 'knickers' as they were then

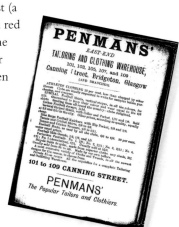

Right: The Celtic team is pictured in 1888 wearing the club's first kit, which featured white shirts supplied by Penmans'

Willie Maley (right) played in Celtic's first game and later became the club's manager. As a hosier and draper by trade, his company may also have supplied some of the team's early kits

known) were black with a thin stripe down each side, and the players wore an assortment of socks, most often green and black hoops.

Willie Maley, who played in Celtic's first game and went on to manage the club from 1897 until 1940, wrote in his 1939 book, *The Story of the Celtic*, that these first strips "were presented to the club by Penman Bros, then the big drapers and clothiers at Bridgeton Cross". Maley also made reference to a different strip that was worn in trial games prior to the Penmans' kits arriving, but no details of its style or colour have ever been unearthed. It is a point of eternal frustration and deep regret among Celtic historians and collectors alike that there are no known surviving examples of these early relics.

William Penman had set up the clothiers bearing his family name around 1878 and soon the business was housed in the largest warehouse of its type in the East End of Glasgow. As well as supplying Celtic's first-ever kits, Penman Brothers were also early shareholders in the club.

Penmans advertised themselves as "the popular tailors and clothiers" of Glasgow's East End, where their warehouse was situated at 101-109 Canning Street, Bridgeton. However, they specialised in sports-specific jerseys, even though these were essentially traditional dress shirts. "Clubs are kindly requested to write for samples before purchasing," explained one newspaper advert, before providing their prices – "Special football shirts, vertical stripes, in all the colours, for 3/11. Blue serge football knickers with hip pocket, 2/3 and 2/6."

The reference to vertical stripes is interesting. Football shirts featuring this pattern did not become widely available until 1883, when they were very much in vogue and were adopted by many clubs. Horizontal stripes, or hoops, was a style more associated with rugby. It is perhaps no surprise, then, that when Celtic adopted their first green and white kit, the classic club colours appeared in vertical stripes rather than hoops.

As very few photographs exist from this early period, it is not known exactly when Celtic switched to their new look. However, one rare image proves that on 16th February 1889 Celtic lined up in green and white stripes to face Corinthians in a

"When Celtic adopted their first green and white kit, the classic club colours appeared in vertical stripes rather than hoops"

GLASGOW LEAGUE CHAMPIONSHIP
1898 1899
CELTIC F.C.

AGNEW & SON, THE EXPERT PHOTOGRAPHISTS.   COPYRIGHT.   45 BRIDGE STREET, GLASGOW.

D. FRIEL, *Trainer.*   T. HINES.   J. BELL.   W. ORR.   H. MARSHALL.   J. HODGE.   D. RUSSELL.   A. KING   W. MALEY, *Secy. and Manager.*
        J. DOCHERTY.   P. SOMERS.   J. WELFORD.   J. CAMPBELL.   D. STORRIER.   B. BATTLES.   A. M'MAHON.   R. DAVIDSON.
                    P. GILHOOLY.   D. M'ARTHUR.

CELTIC FOOTBALL CLUB (TEAM 1898-99.)
WINNERS OF SCOTTISH CUP, GLASGOW CHARITY CUP, AND GLASGOW LEAGUE CHAMPIONSHIP.

The formidable 1898/99 Celtic side is pictured in the green-and-white-striped kit which was worn until 1903

friendly match at the Kennington Oval in south London. This strip was accompanied by black shorts – which extended below the knee – and black socks.

Celtic won their first silverware wearing the green and white stripes when they demolished Cowlairs 6–1 in the Glasgow North-Eastern Football Association Cup final on 11th May 1889. They followed this

up with their first 'major' trophy win on Valentine's Day 1891, by virtue of a 4–0 Glasgow Cup victory over Third Lanark. Celtic also won their first Scottish Cup wearing this kit when they met Queen's Park in a replay held at Ibrox Park on 9th April 1892.

Celtic continued to wear the stripes until 1903, albeit with various button or laced collar variations. The kit also saw the reintroduction of white shorts, which had been briefly used during the 1891/92 season but replaced the black ones permanently from the 1899 Scottish Cup Final onwards. Celtic have worn white shorts ever since.

The devastating Celtic Park fire of 9th May 1904 completely destroyed the stadium's grandstand and pavilion, including all of its contents. Many records and artefacts were lost in that fire, including details of Celtic's early kit supply arrangements. William Penman lived until 18th July 1913, and it is possible that Penman Brothers continued to provide the kits until that time. Another potential supplier was Celtic's first manager, Willie Maley, who operated his own drapers and hosiery business from 1894 until 1901, initially at 155 Gallowgate, then at 30 Saltmarket from 1895. An advert from 8th October 1895 announced that Willie Maley was "the largest athletic outfitter in Scotland".

What we do know for certain is that on the first day of the 1903/04 season, Celtic took the field wearing green and white hoops for the first time. Football historians and lovers of the game often like to romanticise the origins of football club shirts. But with fledgling clubs in these early days of football frequently changing their colours, the reality is that often the reasons a particular shirt was chosen prove far more mundane and practical than might be hoped.

What we do know for certain is that Celtic had a

An advertisement for Willie Maley's outfitters promoting kit, boots and footballs, as well as cricket, cycling and swimming equipment

terrible season in 1902/03. Is it possible that a fresh start was deemed desirable? The fact that it would be a unique design amongst the major Scottish clubs may very well also have appealed to those charged with running Celtic, given its special origins and purpose.

It is possible that the original Hibernian green-and-white-hooped jersey was an influence, although this seems unlikely since the relationship between the two clubs was now markedly less cordial than it had been in 1887. Indeed, Hibernian only wore their green and white hoops for two seasons before switching to an all-green shirt in 1879, only adding white sleeves in the 1930s in tribute to Herbert Chapman's great Arsenal side.

What is certain is that the often-quoted legend that Celtic got the idea for their iconic hooped jerseys from the junior club St Anthony's, located in Govan just a few hundred yards from Ibrox Park, is a myth. Alastair Hay, the St Anthony's historian, points out that Celtic first wore their hoops in 1903 and that the junior club did not play their first match until 1904. Indeed, St Anthony's are thought to have initially worn

Black shorts were usually worn with Celtic's striped shirts until 1899

"The press commented that the hoops made Celtic 'look faster and fitter'"

Above: Celtic in their trademark hoops ahead of the 1905/06 season, having adopted them in 1903

Right: FA Lumley's Athletic Stores was just one of the outfitters advertising themselves as suppliers of jerseys to Celtic during the early 1900s

red jerseys and Hay believes that in fact the first set of hoops worn by St Anthony's were probably cast-offs provided by Celtic.

Whatever the reasons for it, the hoops made their debut on 15th August 1903 in the opening league match of the 1903/04 season, when Celtic overcame Partick Thistle 2-1. Alec Bennett became the first Celtic player to score in the green and white hoops, while Jimmy McMenemy netted the winner. The press commented that the hoops made Celtic "look faster and fitter", a description that certainly would have pleased Willie Maley, who was trying at that time to build a new, youthful team. Coincidentally, on the very same day that Celtic wore the hoops

for the first time, so too did East Fife, who played their debut match in a similar green-and-white-hooped strip.

It is believed that the first hooped Celtic kit was supplied by Glasgow sports outfitters TRC Charlton. The company's ad in *The Scottish Referee* newspaper in 1908, under the heading "FACTS! FACTS! TRUTH! TRUTH!", stated: "The Green and White jerseys worn by the Celtic Football team last season, and for several seasons previously, were supplied by TRC Charlton, Athletic Outfitter, 20 and 101 Argyle Street, Glasgow."

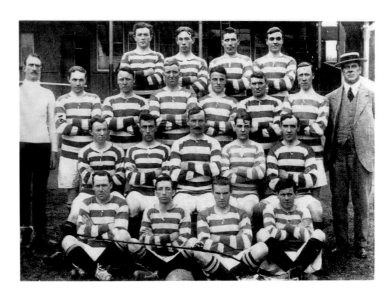

However, on the same page in the same newspaper there is an advert for a rival outfitter, FA Lumley's Athletic Stores – who had offices in Edinburgh (127 Leith Street) and Glasgow (12 Sauchiehall Street) – which stated: "PROMINENT CUP FIGHTERS AND LEADING LEAGUE CLUBS LIKE CELTIC, RANGERS, CLYDE & Co. WEAR FA LUMLEY'S RENOWNED FOOTBALL OUTFITS."

Since at this time clubs purchased their kit from such suppliers, it is quite possible that sets of jerseys were at some point acquired from both companies. Certainly, the club's run of success after adopting the hoops – Celtic went on to win six league championships in a row from 1905-1910, during which time they also won two Scottish Cups, five Glasgow Cups and two Glasgow Charity Cups – appears to have had the Glasgow sports outfitters falling over themselves to associate themselves with the now illustrious Celtic.

The club's accumulation of silverware at this time, as well as the widespread admiration for the team and their striking jerseys, cemented the hoops – accompanied by white shorts and black socks – as the renowned Celtic jersey, and from its inception in 1903 it remained relatively unchanged until 1936. The round-neck collar was laced or buttoned up the front, or right of centre, and the black socks sometimes had the addition of green and/or white hoops to the tops, but the differences were minimal. A collar did make another appearance around 1919 but it was gone again by 1921. In some matches a combination of styles was worn, indeed the team photo of 1920/21 shows an assortment of both jerseys (collared and round-necked) on display among the Celtic squad. In comparison, the team photo of the following season shows the players in alternate home and all-green away jerseys.

Sadly, there are no known surviving examples of any of these early jerseys. Like all clubs in these early days of football, Celtic had to purchase their own kit and once shirts had been worn by the first team they would have been handed down to the reserves, used as training kit and eventually cut up and used for rags to clean the players' boots and the dressing room. The idea that these would one day become historic items of memorabilia would simply not have occurred to anyone at the club.

Celtic have been known for penny-pinching at times during their history, but in fairness making use of playing kit until it literally fell apart was common practice at the time. More unusually, it is believed that for many years Celtic relied upon the charitable assistance of the nuns at Dalbeath's Good Shepherd for the laundry of the

Above: The Celtic team pictured in 1913, with players wearing several different versions of the hoops

Left: Variations in the Celtic jersey in the first half of the century can be clearly seen on cigarette cards from the era

Good Shepherd for the laundry of the kit and the responsibility of ensuring that the green and white hoops remained as resplendent as possible.

The early history of Celtic's jersey shows the club's loyalty to its heritage. Many teams changed their early club colours through the passage of time, including Dundee United, who wore green when they were known as Dundee Hibernian; and Manchester United, who wore green and yellow as Newton Heath. Celtic can justifiably feel a huge sense of pride that they have remained true to their original Irish identity for more than 130 unbroken years.

For many years, even Celtic's away kits were green and white, and these were only ever worn when there was a genuine clash.

In the 1921/22 team group picture *(above right)*, half of the Celtic players are modelling a green away jersey with a white collar, white or black shorts, and black socks. This was largely the look of the change kit right up to the introduction of the famous 'Shamrock' jerseys *(see page 30)* in 1926, with a few exceptions: an Airdrieonians-style white half-diamond 'v' appeared on the top half of the 1919/20 jersey; a white horizontal band appeared on the 1922/23 shirt; the 1926/27 effort was quartered in green and white, which made it look like a jockey's jersey; and in 1929/30 the club had a white change shirt. Sadly, there are no known examples of any of these jerseys in existence.

Celtic's away jerseys would also have been worn when they pitched the reserve side against the first team in pre-season trial

J. Connor, D. Pratt, J. M'Knight, C. Shaw, J. Cassidy.
W. Quinn (Trainer), H. Hilley, A. M'Nair, Jas. M'Stey, J. Dodds, W. M'Stey, T. M'Inally, S. Glasgow, J. Gilchrist.
J. M'Farlane, F. Collins, J. M'Master, A. M'Atee, J. M'Kay, P. Gallacher, J. Murphy, A. M'Lean, W. Cringan.
Agnew, Photo.   **CELTIC FOOTBALL CLUB, 1921-1922.**   *98 Trongate.*

matches. These encounters, which could make-or-break a player's season, were billed as the 'Stripes' (as the hoops were then referred to) against the 'Greens'.

All of this would change much later, of course, particularly with modern away kits, which have introduced gold, silver, yellow and even pink to the Celtic jersey – concepts that would have been unthinkable in the early years. However, it is the green and white hoops that sets Celtic apart in the landscape of world football.

Over the following 300 pages you will find the most extensive collection of Celtic jerseys ever collated – all of them either match worn or match prepared – including every version of the home jersey (and nearly all of the change shirts) from the 1930s to the present day. Featuring shirts worn by some of the club's greatest players in some of its most famous games, *The Celtic Jersey* offer a unique perspective on the wonderful history of this most famous club.

A photograph of the 1921/22 Celtic squad that has been colourised, with some players wearing the hoops and others wearing the all-green away jersey

"The early history of Celtic's jersey shows the club's loyalty to its heritage"

CHAPTER TWO
DOUBLE DIAMOND WORKS WONDERS
UMBRO 1936-63

THE START OF SOMETHING SPECIAL

Celtic began wearing Umbro jerseys during the 1930s, embarking on a fruitful partnership with the kit manufacturer that lasted nearly 70 years

The early football shirts were essentially modified gentlemen's dress shirts, but as the game expanded more modern practices were introduced and specialist sports kit manufacturers began to emerge.

One of the first specialist sports garment manufacturers was Bukta (formed in Stockport in 1879), but by the 1930s one company emerged as the leading player. Formed in 1924 as Humphrey Brothers Clothing Ltd, Umbro, as they came to be known – the 'Um' coming from Humphrey and 'Bro' from founding brothers Harold and Wallace – combined pioneering product development with clever marketing to rapidly dominate the football shirt market.

Umbro's football shirts were made from a knitted, shrink-resistant Peruvian cotton which they branded 'Tangeru' and, being lighter and more comfortable than most other jerseys on the market, they were quickly adopted by many football clubs. The company supplied several English FA Cup-winning teams, including Manchester City in 1934, and were quick to advertise the fact. Umbro's main interest was the business of selling kit to amateur clubs and schools, so being able to boast about supplying the top teams was crucial to their sales strategy.

However, it is important to remember that at this time, and for several decades to come, there were no kit deals as such. Football clubs purchased their kit from local sports distributors, selecting styles from the kit companies' catalogues. Consequently, over a period of time they might wear kit from more than one manufacturer, depending on favoured style or availability of stock.

It is not known exactly when Celtic jumped aboard the Umbro bandwagon, but we do know that by the 1930s the club was purchasing the Manchester company's kit via local retailer The Sportsman's Emporium Ltd of 103 St Vincent Street, Glasgow. Initially

> "Umbro combined pioneering product development with clever marketing to rapidly dominate the football shirt market"

The collar label from Jimmy Delaney's 1945 jersey (see overleaf) includes details of The Sportsman's Emporium, the outfitters through whom Celtic purchased their kit at this time

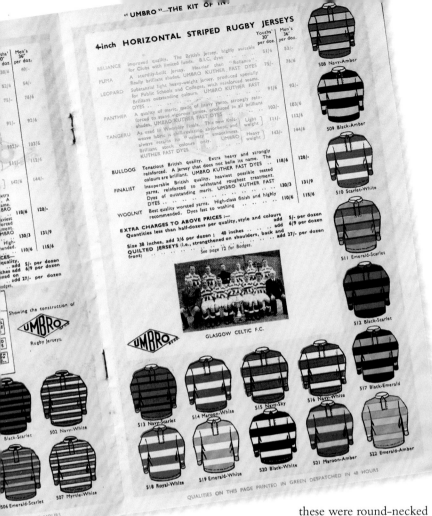

Glasgow Celtic F.C., winners Scottish Cup, 1937, photographed in their "UMBRO" Kit

Above: A page from the 1937 Umbro catalogue confirms that Celtic were wearing 'horizontal striped' jerseys designed for rugby

Above right: Celtic's 1937 Scottish Cup-winning team in their 'Umbro kit'

these were round-necked jerseys with three buttons, and this is the style of the oldest surviving hooped jersey in existence – worn on the club's maiden tour of America in 1931. This historic Umbro jersey was sold at auction in May 2011 for £3,000.

At some point during the 1936/37 season, however, Celtic switched to a version of their now famous jersey with seven green hoops and a white rugby-style collar and cuffs (although the cuffs may have been green on early versions). It was wearing this style that the Bhoys won the Scottish Cup in 1937, and the Umbro catalogue produced later that year features a photograph of the Celtic team group with the trophy. Interestingly, the photograph appears in the section advertising '4-inch Horizontal Striped Rugby Jerseys', and it appears that Celtic were purchasing

'Emerald and white' kit primarily designed for the oval ball game. Hoops were still very much considered a feature of rugby shirts at this time, with vertical stripes being the style more associated with football.

Celtic wore the collared version of the hoops for the 1937 Scottish Cup win, and the style remained almost completely unchanged for 27 years, although very few examples have survived. It is difficult to comprehend now, but the future historical or financial value of the players' jerseys was not considered. At a time when money was always tight, first-team shirts that were past their best would be passed down to the reserve, third and youth teams and eventually used in training. They would be repaired when necessary until finally cut up and used as cloths for cleaning boots or the dressing rooms. Much to the dismay of Celtic collectors around the world, there are, therefore, very few known examples of pre-1960s jerseys in existence.

Umbro would continue to supply Celtic with kit for the next 69 years or so, and the name is synonymous with some of the most glorious moments and players in the club's illustrious history.

HOME 1936-63

Match worn by Jimmy Delaney

The shirt featured on these pages is the oldest surviving Celtic jersey to appear in this book. It was worn by winger Jimmy Delaney in a series of unofficial wartime matches in 1945.

This rugby-style Umbro jersey was worn by the club for nearly 30 years, remaining virtually unchanged from its introduction in 1936 until 1963. The design generally included seven green hoops and a sturdy buttoned-up collar. White shorts and green stockings with one or two white bands or hoops were worn with this shirt style.

The featured jersey is shorter than later versions of this style, incorporating just six hoops, and at some point the sleeves have been cut off. It was obtained by the current owner's father directly from the Delaney family.

Jimmy Delaney first appeared for Celtic on 18th August 1934. Manager Willie Maley introduced the 20-year-old winger into a side that boasted the goalscoring prowess of Jimmy McGrory who, nearly 90 years later, remains the club's most prolific marksman.

Delaney was part of the side which won Celtic's first league title in a decade in 1936. A year later Celtic and Delaney played – wearing the new rugby-style jerseys – in front of a world-record crowd for a club match when 147,365 turned up at Hampden Park to watch them defeat Aberdeen 2-1 in the Scottish Cup Final. Maley then led Celtic to another league title during the 1937/38 season and on to the Empire Exhibition Trophy where, following a 1-0 defeat of Everton, the Bhoys were crowned 'Champions of Britain'.

Disaster struck for Delaney in April 1939 when, during a league encounter against Arbroath, he badly broke his arm. The jersey he was wearing, which had to be cut from him to allow his injury to be treated, was sold at Christie's for £564 in 2002.

Following this career-threatening injury, Delaney faced a lengthy period on the sidelines. Then came the Second World War, during which he worked in the mining industry while continuing to make appearances for the club in wartime matches. His wholehearted performances were one of the few highlights for Celtic during those bleak years.

Jimmy Delaney takes on
Rangers with the long sleeves
of his jersey rolled up

CORONATION CUP FINAL 1953

Match worn by Neilly Mochan

The hoops featured on these pages were worn by Neilly Mochan, Celtic's future kitman, in the famous Coronation Cup Final against Hibernian in 1953. Highly unusually in these times of post-war austerity, after the match Mochan was able to keep his full kit – including his shorts and socks – and these wonderfully preserved items mark the start of his extensive memorabilia collection, which forms the backbone of this book.

Longer than the Jimmy Delaney wartime shirt featured on the previous pages and incorporating seven green hoops, the fact that this Umbro jersey can be specifically dated to such a famous match makes it uniquely historically significant.

The Coronation Cup was staged in 1953 to celebrate Elizabeth II's accession to the throne, and Celtic – who had endured a miserable season in 1952/53 – surprised everybody with sparkling victories against Arsenal (1-0) and Manchester United (2-1) en route to the final against Hibernian. The Hampden Park showpiece on 20th May 1953 was played in front of a crowd of 117,060, which witnessed a famous 2-0 victory. Neilly Mochan opened the scoring with a 30-yard strike that is widely regarded as one of fiercest shots ever struck by a Celtic forward.

It is not known if Mochan – who had only signed three days before Celtic's first match in this competition – was officially presented with his kit or obtained it some other way, but we do know that it was later passed down to his son, Neil Junior, with the rest of his vast collection.

Left: Talismanic defender Bobby Evans holds the Coronation Cup

Below: The socks and shorts worn by Neilly Mochan during the final

AWAY 1952-65

THE 'SHAMROCK' JERSEY

Match worn by Paddy Crerand

The 'Shamrock' or 'Political' jersey worn between 1952 and 1965 is one of the most celebrated shirts from Celtic's early history. Undoubtedly the style's popularity stems from its proud statement of Irish identity at a time when anti-Irish sentiment was rife in Glasgow and beyond.

Because of the club's roots, naturally enough the shamrock has been a recurring motif throughout Celtic's history. In 1892, the Irish patriot Michael Davitt (an Irish nationalist and founder of the National Land League) visited Celtic Park and famously laid a sod of earth containing a "splendid bunch of shamrocks" – that he had brought from Donegal – in the centre of the pitch at the newly built stadium.

"Mr Davitt said that he was delighted to have the honour of laying the centre sod of the new park which belonged to the Celtic club," it was reported. "He could assure them that the prowess of the Celts was well known and appreciated by their countrymen beyond the sea, who were proud to witness the efforts of an Irish team in Scotland."

Shamrock motifs did appear in the foyer at Celtic Park and for many years adorned the corner flags at the club's home – until they were banned following a UEFA directive in the early 1970s and ended up in Rod Stewart's back garden – but for the vast majority of Celtic's history the famous hoops have not been adorned with any kind of badge. Indeed, with few other clubs playing in green, there was little need for Celtic to change their strip (apart from fixtures against Kilmarnock and Greenock Morton). On those rare occasions, Celtic normally wore their predominantly green away kit.

The 1926/27 season, however, saw the first appearance of a plain white away jersey which featured a large green shamrock badge, and the design was also worn during a handful of games in 1931.

After the end of the Second World War the design resurfaced, although this time with a green collar. In February 1946, right-

Back row (L. to R.)—W. O'Neill, Gemmell, Clark, McCarron, McKay, Madden, Haffey, Brankin, F. Brogan.
Middle row (L. to R.)—Halpin, Kennedy, Young, Hughes, Lawson, Divers, Cullen, Price, Cushley, Parks, G. O'Neill, McNamee, J. Brogan.
Front row (L. to R.)—Manager McGrory, McCallum, Chalmers, Brady, Turner, Lennox, McNeill, Gnaulati, Gallacher, Johnstone, Murdoch, Trainer Rooney.

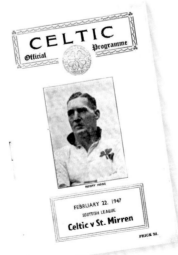

Top: The 1963/64 team photo shows the players wearing a mixture of hoops and Shamrock jerseys

Left: Bobby Hogg appears on the cover of a 1947 match programme wearing the original white-sleeved version of the shirt

back Bobby Hogg, who had been a member of the famous Empire Exhibition Cup-winning team of 1938, appeared on the cover of the match programme, arms-crossed and stern-faced, wearing a white jersey with green collar and shamrock on the left breast. During the 1948/49 season the green-collared design resurfaced, although it was only used on a few occasions.

It is the third version of this shirt – which featured the addition of green sleeves – that has become known as the cult 'Shamrock' or 'Political' jersey.

The jersey was first seen on 17th May 1952 in a friendly match against Belfast Celtic in Belfast, with the fact that it was worn by the home team leading many to believe that it was originally a Belfast Celtic kit that had been gifted to Celtic. However, this theory has recently been disproved.

"The friendly played in May 1952 in Belfast was a one-off charity game and, having folded in 1949, it was Belfast Celtic's first match in three years," explains Celtic author and historian Ian McCallum. "The team was cobbled together over the week previous to the game. I've seen a photo of them training in their traditional green and white hoops prior to the match. So I think it likely that Celtic brought that Shamrock strip with them from Glasgow, and lent it to the home side to avoid a clash."

Martin Flynn of the Belfast Celtic Society Committee is of the same view. "As far as I'm aware, this was the only time Belfast Celtic wore this jersey," he says.

The confusion is compounded by the fact that Celtic did not wear the Shamrock jersey in a competitive match until 1955, although it had made another appearance on the cover of the match programme for the league match against Clyde on 12th September 1953. The jersey finally saw action when Celtic faced Kilmarnock in a league game on 8th January 1955 with the *Evening Times* report running with the headline: "Tully Trick In A New Strip, Celtic Just Make It."

Eminent Celtic historian and author Pat Woods points out that: "At this time Kilmarnock matches were the only occasions which necessitated a strip change [Kilmarnock normally wore blue and white hoops]. But Kilmarnock were not in the First Division during the period from 1947/48 to 1953/54, and did not play Celtic in any competition during that time."

The Shamrock jersey was worn for the final time in a Scottish Cup tie against Kilmarnock on 6th March 1965. This 3-2 victory was Jimmy McGrory's final game in charge of Celtic, which means that the Shamrock shirts were never worn by a team managed by Jock Stein.

The jersey was seen by many as a controversial and provocative choice of playing strip. At a time when the notorious 'No Blacks, No Dogs, No Irish' attitude was commonplace in Glasgow and throughout the UK, large sections of Scottish society were opposed to Celtic celebrating their Irish patriotism by adorning a bold shamrock on their jersey.

Even amongst the Celtic support, the style received a mixed reception. Many felt that there was too much white in the strip and criticised the contrasting sleeves design, comparing it unfavourably with Arsenal and Hibernian. As time has passed, however, it has become an iconic shirt and many supporters yearn for its return.

The match worn version featured on these pages belongs to Celtic Football Club, whose records confirm that the jersey was worn by Paddy Crerand. It is an unusual version of the shirt as it has a white collar. Ex-Celtic goalkeeper John Fallon remembers that the club had two sets of Shamrock strips – the green collars were worn by the first team while the white collars were for the reserve side.

Like all jerseys from this era, surviving examples are extremely rare and something of a holy grail to collectors. On 13th March 2020 a match worn example from the Stevie Chalmers collection was sold at McTear's Auctioneers in Glasgow for £7,000.

Right: Charlie Tully (left) leads Celtic out against Belfast Celtic – wearing kit loaned by their opponents – in May 1952

Right: Paddy Crerand on the ball against Kilmarnock in the Scottish Cup in 1965, the final appearance of the Shamrock jersey

NORTH AMERICA TOUR 1957

Match worn by Neilly Mochan

Throughout the first 50 or 60 years of the club's history, Celtic's players were accustomed to pulling on heavyweight hooped jerseys with long sleeves that were sturdy enough to see them through the cold, wet Scottish winters, even doing so when the weather was warmer at the start and finish of each season. In 1957, however, the club embarked on a post-season tour to North America and took with them a set of short-sleeved, lightweight shirts to better suit the hot and humid summer conditions they would face.

Once again manufactured by Umbro and identical to the usual hooped shirt in every way other than the shorter sleeves and 'Light Weight' material, the jerseys that sailed with the Celtic party from Southampton on 8th May 1957 were quite possibly the first set of short-sleeved shirts that the club ever purchased.

On arrival in North America, the tourists – led by newly appointed captain Bertie Peacock – played eight games in three weeks in New York, Philadelphia, St Louis, Vancouver, San Francisco, Toronto and Montreal.

The schedule included victories over Philadelphia Uhrik Truckers (4-0), Hapoel Tel Aviv (2-1), St Louis All-Stars (3-0) and a San Francisco XI (5-0). However, the Scottish League Cup winners found things more difficult against a Danny Blanchflower-inspired Tottenham Hotspur, who inflicted three defeats upon them (4-3, 6-3 and 3-1) before Jimmy McGrory's men were able to restore some pride with a 2-0 victory over the north London side.

Neilly Mochan netted a brace in that final tour match against Spurs in Montreal, following which Celtic are said to have gifted their entire kit to a local Celtic supporters club, with the hoops being worn thereafter by Montreal Celtic. Forever the hoarder, however, and perhaps unsurprisingly considering his impressive 10-goal haul on the tour in which he featured in all eight games, Mochan kept his jersey as a keepsake, which means this historic shirt has survived.

Above: Neilly Mochan (left) is pictured following a match on Celtic's 1957 tour of North America on which he scored 10 goals in eight matches

Right: The collar label from this 'Light Weight' Umbro jersey, including The Sportsman's Emporium distributor label

LEAGUE CUP FINAL 1957

Match worn by Neilly Mochan

Next to the European Cup Final of 1967, perhaps no Celtic match arouses such a feeling of pride as the League Cup Final of 19th October 1957. On that magical afternoon at Hampden Park, Celtic defeated Rangers 7-1. 'Defeated' is probably the mildest word that can be applied to the events of that day. The headline in one popular Sunday newspaper asserted, "It Could Have Been Ten!" and in the eyes of many who were there that was certainly an understatement.

The fact that we are able to present a jersey that was worn in such a historic match is once again thanks to Neilly Mochan, who scored two of Celtic's seven goals. As we know, unlike many of his contemporaries, Mochan meticulously saved any jerseys that he was allowed to keep and after the match, with the players having been presented with their jerseys by the club in acknowledgement of their triumph, he held on to his cup final hoops. We know for certain that this is the jersey from this famous match because of the small bloodstains still visible on the back of the jersey, which were the result of a boil on Mochan's back bursting during the match.

Apart from this somewhat gruesome detail – passed down to Mochan's son, Neil Junior, who would later inherit his father's collection – this Umbro 'Tangeru' jersey is identical to the previous long-sleeved hooped shirts previously featured in this book.

Prior to the final – for which Celtic took to the field in their classic 'rugby-style' home kit of the period, their green and white hoops with white shorts and green socks resplendent – there had been little indication of the hammering they were about to inflict on their fiercest rivals. Celtic had enjoyed the better of the earlier contests between the two sides that season but Rangers were probably slight favourites with the bookies.

Within minutes of the kick-off, however, Celtic had seized the initiative: Charlie Tully at outside-right was confusing Eric Caldow; Neilly Mochan on Celtic's left was overpowering Bobby Shearer; Bobby Collins was full of running and – for such a little man – yet again proved a powerful presence on the pitch; Billy McPhail, as hoped, was winning the aerial duel with Rangers' new signing

Above: Rangers were simply outclassed by a rampant Celtic side in the 1957 Scottish League Cup Final

Left: This jersey can be identified as the one from this famous match by the small blood stain on the back, caused by a burst boil

Johnny Valentine; and the prolific Sammy Wilson was looking to get on the end of every knockdown.

After 20 minutes of domination – during which both Tully and Collins (with a piledriver from 30 yards) had struck the woodwork with George Niven helpless in the Rangers goal – a breakthrough finally came. McPhail won yet another header and Wilson was perfectly placed to stroke the ball home from 15 yards. Then, only a minute from the interval, Mochan left both Ian McColl and Shearer in his wake, cut in and from a narrow angle found the net with a typical hard-driven shot.

Rangers, with the wind now behind them, were expected to fight back in the second half but Celtic were in irresistible form, and nobody more so than Willie Fernie at right-half. Time after time this elegant player – who had originally plied his trade as an inside-forward – would stride out of defence, leaving Rangers' hard men Harold Davis and Sammy Baird struggling behind him, and play a crucial pass to his forwards. Collins, too, was in inspired form.

McPhail headed in Celtic's third goal on 53 minutes and smashed in a fourth 14 minutes later with Rangers' defenders in total disarray. Mochan, he of the trademark explosive shot, promptly hammered in his second goal of the game on 75 minutes. The rout was on.

The Celtic supporters, ensconced in the distant King's Park End of Hampden, were almost delirious by the time McPhail shrugged off the despairing Valentine to complete his hat-trick on 80 minutes. Almost unbelievably, it arguably should have been more at this point: every Celtic thrust threatened to end with a panic-stricken Rangers defender putting the ball into their own net.

In the very last minute Celtic were awarded a penalty kick. Willie Fernie, appointed to take it, shrugged his shoulders, studied Niven in goal, decided the goalkeeper's cap lying in the back of the net made a good target, stepped forward and sent the bunnet spinning with his shot.

It should probably be mentioned Rangers scored – albeit when Celtic were already 3-0 up and centre-half Bobby Evans was off the field receiving treatment for an injury. But they were frankly never anything less than second best throughout.

Sadly for those fans not at the game, a technical hitch meant that none of the second-half goals were ever seen by a television audience. Nevertheless, for Celtic supporters of a certain vintage this was a 'JFK moment' since without exception those who were not in the crowd know exactly where they were when they heard the news.

Over the years the result has inspired numerous terrace songs, including, within days, the adaptation of Harry Belafonte's catchy hit record of that year, *Island in the Sun* to *Hampden in the Sun*. The song also references the fact that in 1957 Russia had taken the lead in the 'Space Race' with the launch of Sputnik 1, Earth's first man-made satellite, much to the consternation of the West.

> *Twinkle, twinkle little Sputnik*
> *You are sure a dirty trick*
> *Up above the world so high*
> *Making zig-zags in the sky*
> *How the hell can people sleep*
> *When all night long goes 'Beep, beep, beep'?*
> *Telling every Tim in Heaven*
> *Rangers one and Celtic seven*

Books were also written on the game, most notably by Peter Burns and Pat Woods (inevitably titled *Oh, Hampden in the Sun*), and tales of the post-match celebrations developed a life of their own. And whilst the players were, unusually, allowed to keep their jerseys after the match, Neilly Mochan's is the only known survivor in existence.

Left: Willie Fernie's pinpoint penalty completes Celtic's 7-1 triumph

Left: Neilly Mochan's medal from the famous League Cup triumph

THE NUMBERS GAME

For many years Celtic was the only team in Britain to wear shirts without numbers on the back, with the club holding out for as long as possible to keep the sacred hoops untarnished

Shirt numbering for the purpose of player identification was formally introduced into British football by the English FA in 1939, the concept having been pioneered by revolutionary Arsenal manager Herbert Chapman.

When football restarted after the Second World War, the Scottish FA decided to follow the lead of their counterparts south of the border. However, one prominent club declined to participate, and for the next 50 years or so Celtic's hooped home shirts remained free of numbers.

Other teams whose traditional kits featured hoops or stripes were able to incorporate player numbers by using a third colour or a rectangular patch background, but Celtic insisted that such tampering with their classic green-and-white-hooped jerseys would be a sacrilegious act. Despite pressure from the football authorities and regular criticism from those who inhabited the Celtic Park press box – whose profession relied upon being able to correctly identify players – the club refused to give in.

Robert 'Bob' Kelly – Celtic chairman between 1947-1971 – insisted: "When Celtic can

find a system of numbering without spoiling the appearance of their jerseys, they will be glad to do so."

Cyril Horne of the *Glasgow Herald*, a personal friend of the chairman, backed his stance. "Numbers?" he wrote on 9th December 1952. "The massive McPhail is McPhail to everyone whether he has a number on his back or not; no one can mistake the magnificent enthusiasm of Evans or the countenance that becomes florid the more he urges on his colleagues; Smith of Hibernian would surely know Fallon irrespective of whether that first-time tackler had a halo round his head; Collins when he returns to the Parkhead first team will again be recognised for his Tom Thumb appearance as well for his mighty shooting; and Tully, we are sure, would give up the game if all his friends and foes did not take note of his desire to be different with number or without."

Why were Celtic so reluctant to number their home shirts (the club's plain white, green or yellow away shirts carried numbers)? Certainly, their famous hooped jerseys were among the most iconic and revered in world football, and horizontally hooped jerseys are notoriously

"When Celtic can find a system of numbering without spoiling the appearance of their jerseys, they will be glad to do so"

Bob Kelly, Celtic Chairman

Right: Keen to maintain the integrity of the sacred green and white hoops, in 1960 Celtic opted to place numbers on the players' shorts rather than their jerseys

Below left: Celtic chairman Bob Kelly was a staunch defender of the club's refusal to tarnish the famous hooped shirt with numbers

difficult to combine with vertical numbers, but other teams managed to do it and the club's stubbornness was difficult to fathom.

Bob Kelly was an autocratic chairman. His father had been the club's first captain, and later Celtic chairman, and as a result in childhood the younger Kelly had developed an astonishingly deep bond with the club. Above all, he was known to be a staunch traditionalist. The convenience of spectators was simply not a sufficiently compelling argument to persuade him to accept what was – in his eyes – a radical change.

Desmond White, a fellow director and the club's secretary, backed his chairman, claiming: "Celtic's jersey did not lend itself to numbers." As late as 1960, the directors – aware that change was inevitable – were discussing the matter frequently but could not settle on any acceptable design;

instead, they offered a compromise by placing numbers on the players' shorts, thus preserving the clean, untarnished lines of the most distinctive jersey in football. The team wore numbered shorts for the first time in public on 14th May 1960 for an exhibition game at Parkhead against Sparta Rotterdam, the Dutch champions, at the end of the season. Celtic apparently wasted little time in admiring their new appearance and went on to outclass the visitors 5-1.

Was this experiment successful? It was a considerable improvement, but the numbers (black or green on white shorts) were understandably on the small side and not easy to make out from the stands.

Almost three months later, in a pre-season competition called the Friendship Cup between Scottish and French clubs, Celtic played against Sedan in France on 6th August 1960. For the first time in the club's history the players wore numbers on the backs of the famous hooped jerseys. The experiment could not be considered a success, however. The numbers were described as 'yellow' (they may have in fact been gold) and in the glare of the floodlights they were virtually impossible to decipher. Instead of being a help, the numbers had been an irritating distraction and an aesthetic disaster. To make matters worse, despite fielding a strong side, Celtic were trounced 3-0.

The idea was shelved, and thus the combination of unnumbered shirts and white shorts with green numbers on both the front and back are synonymous with the glorious heyday of the 1960s.

Celtic wore numbers on the back of the hoops for the first time against Sedan in France on 6th August 1960

A pair of No.7 shorts, worn by the great Jimmy Johnstone

"The classic kit combination's finest hour came, of course, during the European Cup Final of 1967"

The classic kit combination's finest hour came, of course, during the European Cup Final of 1967, when its fresh appearance – in contrast to the sombre look of Inter Milan – won over many neutrals even before kick-off. Incidentally, amid the euphoria of Celtic's triumph that day, it is generally forgotten that Inter's manager, Helenio Herrera, had attempted almost literally at the last minute to lodge an official protest about Celtic's numbers appearing on the players' shorts rather than on the backs of their jerseys. Perhaps recognising that this was a cynical ploy to upset their opponents, the UEFA officials dismissed it without too much discussion.

However, times were changing and during the 1975/76 season Celtic were

Billy McNeill leads out Celtic ahead of the 1967 European Cup Final with the number 5 prominent on his shorts, despite a late protest by Inter Milan

Celtic wore numbers in a competitive game for the first time against Boavista of Portugal in the UEFA Cup in 1975

Above: A typical Celtic jersey from the late '70s and early '80s that has been numbered for European competition

Below: When Celtic were ordered to put numbers on their shirts in 1994, initially they were placed on the sleeves

arrival of shirt sponsorship which meant that the hoops were already 'embellished' with the name of double-glazing company CR Smith, and later Peoples Ford.

Everything changed at the start of the 1994/95 season, however, when the Scottish Football League ordered Celtic to place numbers on their shirts after a referee apparently blamed a mix-up over a booking on the absence of a shirt number. Even then, under chief executive Fergus McCann, Celtic still tried to come up with a solution that would leave the hoops relatively unspoiled. When the Celtic players ran out for the opening fixture away to Falkirk at Brockville Park on 13th August 1994 – the managerial debut of Tommy Burns and Billy Stark – their jerseys had small numbers on each sleeve. Celtic drew the match 1-1 thanks to a fine header from the returning Andy Walker, but despite the pleasing effect of the numbers on the sleeves the authorities were having none of it and ordered the club to display the numbers on the backs of its jerseys. The

finally ordered to wear numbered home shirts after UEFA made them compulsory for European competitions. On 5th November 1975, then, Celtic played against Boavista with shirt numbers adorning the famous hoops for the first time in a competitive match. The numbers were black and worn on the back of each jersey, placed on a white patch for clarity, with No.1-11 allocated to the starting players and the substitutes being Nos. 12-16 (although it was permitted to waive the No.13 if a player or club was superstitious).

Celtic advanced to the quarter-final of the competition with a convincing 3-1 win over their Portuguese visitors, and from then on the Celtic shirts worn in European competitions have always featured numbers on the back.

In domestic competitions, however, Celtic continued the tradition of having numbers on the players' shorts only, even after the

"Despite the pleasing effect of the numbers on the sleeves the authorities were having none of it"

Celtic lined up ahead of the 2006 League Cup Final wearing training tops and shorts displaying the No.7 in tribute to the iconic Jimmy Johnstone

numbers were introduced for the match against Rangers at Ibrox a fortnight later and have been in place ever since.

Interestingly, there are two other notable occasions when Celtic have further bent the rules regarding player numbers.

For the first home fixture of the 1973/74 season against Clyde (when the league flag was unfurled yet again) every player – goalkeeper, defenders and attackers alike – wore No.8 on their shorts to commemorate winning eight championships in a row.

More than three decades later, Celtic faced Dunfermline Athletic in the 2006 League Cup Final, and the No.7 was prominently on display. Earlier in the week club legend Jimmy Johnstone had died after a courageous fight against a cruel disease. To honour 'Jinky', the Celtic players came out of the tunnel wearing No.7s on their warm-up jackets and shorts. After the match they changed into a new set of hooped jerseys, all with 'Johnstone' and the No.7 emblazoned on the back, for the trophy presentation.

CHAPTER THREE
THE HEYDAY OF THE HOOPS
UMBRO 1963-76

THE JERSEY OF LEGENDS

The switch to Umbro's new 'Real'-style jerseys in 1963 heralded the arrival of Celtic's glorious heyday

The 'Swinging Sixties' was a decade of immense change, and the monumental shift in fashion that reflected the changes in society had a knock-on effect in football.

In the early 1960s Umbro introduced a brand-new shirt design to their catalogue. The new template featured a round, crew-necked collar, was made from Umbro's shrink-resistant 'Tangeru' cotton, and was initially only available in long sleeves. The style was known as the 'Real' jersey and was styled on the shirts worn by Spanish giants Real Madrid in their famous 7-3 demolition of Eintracht Frankfurt at Hampden Park in 1960, which saw them lift the trophy for the fifth time in the competition's first five years of existence.

Umbro's Real jerseys were quickly adopted by many top teams across Britain and beyond, not least the mighty Real Madrid themselves. They were the height of football fashion and Celtic jumped on the bandwagon in time for the 1963 Scottish Cup Final, finally ditching the by now very old-fashioned 'rugby-style' Umbro jerseys they had worn with distinction since 1936.

Initially worn with green socks with white hoops, the arrival of Jock Stein as Celtic manager coincided with the switch to white socks. It is not known for certain if Stein instigated this change, but as the manager in these days was responsible for the ordering of the team kit it is more than likely that it was his decision. What is certain is that the switch completed a sleek, modern look that would soon become famous the world over.

A Celtic team photo from the 1963/64 season, the first full campaign when Umbro's crew-necked Real jerseys were worn

their main business which was selling playing kit via their catalogue to clubs lower down the football pyramid, including amateur teams and schools.

Terrace's job was made considerably easier by the fact that – unlike every other major professional club – Celtic's jerseys still neither required the application of club crests or shirt numbers. This fact does, however, make the authentication of the few surviving jerseys, as well as matching them with the players who would have worn them, extremely difficult.

Before the 1966 World Cup in England, Umbro offered to supply free kit to every team. Even though in the end only seven – including winners England – took up the offer, the company made huge marketing mileage out of the fact that they were 'supplying' all of the qualifying nations.

As part of their World Cup strategy – and perhaps with a nod forward towards the 1970 tournament to be played in Mexico – Umbro updated the Real template and rebranded it as their new 'Aztec' style. Whilst outwardly almost identical, the Aztec shirts were slightly lighter than the Real ones and the cut was a tighter fit.

It was in Umbro Aztec jerseys that Celtic conquered Europe, and the classic crew-necked, seven-hooped emerald and green jerseys were cemented forever into global football folklore.

For many Celtic supporters and football followers around the world, this is *the* classic Celtic jersey.

Umbro's iconic Aztec range as it appeared in the company's catalogue

"It was in Umbro Aztec jerseys that Celtic conquered Europe"

Although the days of the modern kit deal were still some years away, Celtic's relationship with Umbro was certainly evolving by this time. With no replica kit market to speak of, clubs continued to purchase their favoured kits from the manufacturers and it was the job of Umbro's legendary Scottish rep Jim Terrace to ensure that his clubs were well looked after. For Umbro, it was crucial that they were seen to be suppliers for the big teams to encourage

AWAY 1966-73

Match worn by Billy McNeill

When Jock Stein took over as manager at Celtic Park in March 1965, the club was using two different change tops – the 'Shamrock' jersey and a green shirt with white collar and cuffs. Acknowledging the need to settle on a definitive away kit, in 1966 Stein revealed to the *Celtic View* that the club's change colours would be all-green.

The new all-green jersey (now without the white collar and cuffs) made its debut on 5th November for the 0-0 home draw with St Mirren. In a near-sacrilegious comment to the club's official newspaper, striker John Hughes later admitted that he preferred the change kit to the famous green and white hoops.

The jersey featured here was worn by Billy McNeill – unusually with a No.8, rather than his usual No.5 – when Celtic defeated Kilmarnock 2-0 in the final league match of the 1966/67 season, just 10 days before the European Cup Final. This was centre-half John Cushley's last-ever Celtic match and it is believed that McNeill presented him with this shirt at the end. Cushley went on to become a schoolteacher and this jersey was obtained from one of his former pupils.

This jersey style was used in the home leg of the European Cup quarter-final against Vojvodina in 1967. It also made an appearance at home against Red Star Belgrade in the third round in 1968 when, at half-time with the game poised at a 1-1, Stein promised Jimmy Johnstone – who had a fear of flying – that he wouldn't have to travel for the return leg if he could inspire his side to victory. Jinky duly obliged by scoring two and setting another two up in a 5-1 victory.

The all-green jersey was thought to have been retired at the end of the 1972/73 season. However, it surprisingly re-emerged five years later when Celtic faced Clydebank in the league in April 1978. Neilly Mochan was notorious for hoarding kit, but being able to produce a set of jerseys that hadn't been seen in half a decade was impressive even by the legendary kitman's standards.

Jock Stein is carried shoulder-high by his players – clad in the all-green strip – after their 2-0 victory over Kilmarnock in May 1967. The league title was already Celtic's prior to kick-off and the team would depart for Lisbon in the coming days

EUROPEAN CUP FINAL 1967

When the Celtic and Inter Milan teams emerged from the shadow of the long tunnel and onto the sunlit pitch at the Estadio Nacional in Lisbon on 25th May 1967, the contrast between the two sides was striking.

The Italians – almost uniformly dark-haired and tanned – looked, in Jimmy Johnstone's words, "just like film stars". The Scots, their hair ranging in colour from Bertie Auld's black to Jinky's red, with assorted browns and Billy McNeill's shade of blonde in between, at first sight looked a more ill-assorted bunch.

The contrast extended to the strips that the two sets of players wore as they took to the field. Milan is renowned around the world as being a centre for fashion and Inter's famed blue and black stripes,

The side forever immortalised as 'The Lisbon Lions' line-up on a momentous May afternoon in Lisbon

immaculately tailored and cut, would have done credit to a catwalk. Celtic's altogether simpler green and white hoops, coupled with white shorts and socks, may not have oozed sophisticated continental style but they were about to become equally iconic.

In fact, typically of meticulous manager Jock Stein, considerable thought had gone into Celtic's kit for the final. Acutely aware of the likelihood of warm weather and concerned about the effect the Lisbon conditions might have on the team's all-action style of play, Stein understood the importance of ensuring that the players were provided with kit that would best help them deal with the conditions.

Stein's concern about the impact the un-Glasgow-like weather could have on his players cannot be underestimated. When the team arrived in Portugal he banned them from staying out in the sun at their Lisbon hotel with the words, "If I see one freckle, that man's heading home." He had also insisted that copious quantities of suntan lotion travelled with the team.

Kit suppliers Umbro, having made great marketing mileage from the fact that they had provided England's World Cup winners with their strips the previous summer, were well aware of the commercial benefit of supplying the kit to the first British team to win the European Cup. Umbro rep Jim Terrace therefore pulled out all the stops to

continues on page 56

"Typically of meticulous manager Jock Stein, considerable thought had gone into Celtic's kit for the final"

Billy McNeill becomes the first captain of a British side to lift the European Cup

EUROPEAN CUP
FINAL 1967 JERSEYS

**Match worn from
collection of
Neilly Mochan**

Match spare from
collection of
Neilly Mochan

continued from page 52

provide Celtic with jerseys that would allow the players to perform at their best.

Umbro actually prepared two versions of the famous hoops for the final. Both were short-sleeved and made from the lightweight version of Umbro's 'Tangeru' fabric, but one had a round-neck and the other a v-neck. The players trained in the v-necked version on the day before the final and it is likely that Stein himself made the call on which set of shirts would be worn during the match itself. He settled for the round-necked version which, of course, went on to become the most iconic Celtic jersey of all time. The v-necked shirts were never seen again.

Inter's blue-and-black-striped shirts – complete with Italian shield and gold star to signify winning 10 Serie A titles – were also short-sleeved, although slightly heavier than the Celtic players' hoops. But the contrast in the two teams' styles of play was even more striking than their playing strips, with the Italians' pragmatic, highly defensive *Catenaccio* (which directly translates as 'door-bolt') system up against – in the words of Stein himself – Celtic's "pure, beautiful, inventive football".

The match, of course, has long gone down in sporting folklore. Within six minutes of the kick-off Celtic were a goal down, Jim Craig having felled Renato Cappellini and Alessandro Mazzola scoring the subsequent penalty. After that the Italians sat back and locked the door, trusting in their massed defence to hold out against wave after wave of Celtic attacks. At last, just after the break, a Tommy Gemmell thunderbolt flew past the outstretched hands of Giuliano Sarti in the Inter goal. The strike inspired Celtic to even greater heights, and

the decisive goal came with just six minutes left on the clock when a Bobby Murdoch strike was diverted into the Inter Milan net by Stevie Chalmers, who was promptly buried beneath an avalanche of green and white.

Jubilation followed the final whistle, with John Clark just one of the players whose shirt was torn from his back in the pandemonium of the delirious post-match pitch invasion. Indeed, such was the scale of the on-field celebrations that McNeill had to be guided round the outside of the stadium, through the car park and back through to the front of the stand to be presented with the trophy.

"There is not a prouder man on God's Earth than me at this moment," Stein said after the match. "Winning was important, but it was the way that we won that has filled me with satisfaction."

In the world of the Celtic shirt collectors, a match worn jersey from the 1967 Lisbon final is the Holy Grail, and yet the whereabouts of only a handful of authentic

On the day before the final, Stevie Chalmers and Billy McNeill train in the v-neck version of the hoops that was also prepared for the occasion

"Many of the Celtic players lost their jerseys to jubilant supporters at the final whistle"

shirts worn by the Celtic players during the club's most famous match are actually known.

Many of the Celtic players lost their jerseys to jubilant supporters at the final whistle, but with the team having been offered a fresh set at half-time there were spares in the dressing room and several of the team swapped with their Italian counterparts. Jim Craig swapped with Cappellini; Murdoch with Angelo Domenghini; Bobby Lennox with Tarcisio Burgnich; Bertie Auld with Armando Picchi; Chalmers with Gianfranco Bedin; Johnstone with Giacinto Facchetti; and Gemmell with Sandro Mazzola.

The lack of numbers makes tracking down and authenticating surviving jerseys much harder, but very few have re-surfaced. Ultimately, many of them have simply become lost to the depths of time, although recent research has uncovered the fact that Bertie Auld's jersey is still owned by Armando Picchi's family.

The jersey featured on the previous pages belonged to Neilly Mochan, the trainer and kitman who voyaged on every Celtic European odyssey from 1964 until his death in 1994. In the midst of the post-match chaos, Mochan rescued this jersey from the 'away' dressing room that Celtic had been allocated in Lisbon and brought it home

to Scotland. He never knew which player it had been worn by but the authenticity of these uniquely historic green and white hoops is beyond doubt. Many years later, Mochan Junior obtained the signatures for added posterity.

The Inter Milan No.13 shirt also featured is a spare jersey obtained from the Italians' kitman after the game by Mochan. The Celtic kitman also came home with a No.15 shirt, another spare since only numbers 1–11 were used in the match.

How much a match worn Celtic jersey from this historic occasion might fetch in the modern market is impossible to predict. On 13th March 2020, Bedin's Inter Milan jersey, swapped with Stevie Chalmers, was sold at auction for £19,000. The value of Chalmers' match worn shirt is thought to be double that, although for most Celtic fans an RRP of 'priceless' would be a more accurate figure.

Neilly Mochan's European Cup winners medal, which Jock Stein insisted he received

NEILLY MOCHAN'S 1967 MEMORABILIA

On the sun-drenched afternoon of 25th May 1967, Neilly Mochan was an important part of the wiliest bootroom anywhere on the continent. Jock Stein made sure that Neilly was presented with a winners medal to acknowledge his role in this historic victory. In typical fashion, Mochan also held on to other mementos from that unforgettable European campaign, some of which are on display on these pages.

A whistle used to keep the Lisbon Lions in check during training sessions at Barrowfield

A brooch to commemorate Celtic's five trophies in 1966/67

An ornamental plate, presented by UEFA to celebrate the 1967 European Cup win

A metal plate presented to Celtic by first-round opponents FC Zurich

A blazer presented to Neilly Mochan to wear at the celebrations to mark the 25th anniversary of the Lisbon Lions' triumph

INTERCONTINENTAL CUP 1967

Having overcome Inter Milan in the European Cup Final, Jock Stein's side faced a two-legged tie against Argentinian Copa Libertadores winners Racing Club of Buenos Aires for the prestigious Intercontinental Cup.

More than 80,000 fans packed into Hampden Park for Celtic's 1-0 first-leg victory on 18th October, achieved courtesy of a Billy McNeill header. Jimmy Johnstone finished the game covered in bruises and spit having been ruthlessly targeted by the Argentinians. But this was just a taste of what was to come.

Played a fortnight later in Buenos Aires, the second leg threatened to descend into chaos even before a ball was kicked when Celtic's goalkeeper, Ronnie Simpson, was struck by a missile from the crowd and had to be replaced by John Fallon. The resulting bad-tempered 2-1 defeat meant that a play-off in Uruguay was necessary.

Four days later the infamous 'Battle of Montevideo' saw Celtic lose a vicious match 1-0, with four of Stein's men sent off (to Racing's two) as the match descended into an all-out brawl. Celtic's players were convinced that the referee had been bribed.

Celtic wore their regular, long-sleeved jerseys in the first match at Hampden, with the blood-spattered shirt featured overleaf having been worn by McNeill and later swapped with

The 'Real' Jersey collar label suggests that Billy McNeill's shirt had been well-used prior to the Intercontinental Cup Final, since Umbro had rebranded the template as 'Aztec' in 1966

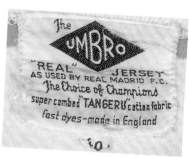

The pennant presented to Racing Club's captain Oscar Martín by Billy McNeill before the first leg at Hampden

WORLD CUP CHAMPIONSHIP 1ST LEG CELTIC RACING CLUB ARGENTINE GLASGOW 18TH OCT. 1967

Racing Club's captain Oscar Martin. Some 40 years later, Celtic shirt collector Jamie Fox traced the jersey to a Buenos Aires-based sports management company. A deal was struck and Jamie retrieved an important part of the club's history. Jamie received the shirt in April 2019, just a few days before McNeill's passing, and describes the experience of pulling on this historic jersey as "magical".

Racing defender Alfio Basile's (foreground) repeated foul play incensed Celtic in the first game

For the second and third matches, played in the warmer climes of Argentina and Uruguay, Celtic wore the short-sleeved, lightweight version of their jersey just as they had done in Lisbon.

Match worn jerseys from this series of matches are extremely rare, especially since many players refused to swap following the ill-tempered games. However, some did survive, and in July 2019 Jimmy Johnstone's jersey from the final game of this three-match series was sold at auction for £4,200.

INTERCONTINENTAL CUP
FINAL 1967 JERSEYS

Match worn by

Billy McNeill

Match worn
by Juan José
Rodríguez

AWAY 1968/69

Match worn by Jimmy Johnstone

Jock Stein had been fond of Celtic's all-green away kit ever since taking the helm in March 1965, and it had fared the team well when needed. But for the home leg of Celtic's first round European Cup tie against Saint-Étienne on 2nd October 1968, a new change kit was required to avoid a clash with the French side's all-green jersey. This prompted the introduction of an all-white Celtic strip – featuring green hoops around the collar and cuffs – which officially became the club's third kit.

Celtic overturned a 2-0 deficit at Celtic Park to win the Saint-Étienne tie 4-2 on aggregate, before eliminating Red Star Belgrade to set up a quarter-final against AC Milan. Many Celtic fans felt that Stein's treble-winners were superior to the side that had lifted the European Cup two seasons previously, but in the end the Italians progressed by a single goal on their way to winning the tournament.

The jersey featured on these pages was worn by Jimmy Johnstone, quite possibly in the match against Saint-Étienne since it was used on very few other occasions.

Johnstone's widow, Agnes, has confirmed that this was 'Jinky's' favourite Celtic kit, because it reminded him of Real Madrid's iconic outfit. The Spaniards held good memories for Johnstone, who had torn them apart during Alfredo Di Stéfano's testimonial in 1967.

With Celtic tending to wear jerseys until they were no longer fit for match action and then handing them down to be used in training – there are even photographs from the 1980s of Neilly Mochan wearing one of these white shirts under his tracksuit – to say that the jersey featured here is rare would be something of an understatement. Thankfully, Mochan did keep this one jersey in his collection and it is the only one of its kind known to have survived.

Jimmy Johnstone was fond of the all-white change strip as it reminded him of the famous Real Madrid kit

AWAY 1970-73

Match worn from the Neilly Mochan collection

This Umbro design introduced in 1970 was the first yellow change strip ever worn by Celtic. It is a colour that has remained in the Celtic jersey palette (both on numerous away kits and recently even as a detail on the home shirts) and the green numbering on the back is another feature that has been seen on numerous subsequent yellow change jerseys.

The shirt featured here appears to have a white collar and cuffs, which would make it different from the all-yellow jerseys worn sporadically in matches from 1970 to 1973. However, on close inspection it is evident that the colour has simply been washed out of them over time. Neilly Mochan often wore older shirts under his tracksuit when employed as a trainer and kitman in the Celtic dugout, and this shirt has evidently been well-worn following its use as a player's jersey.

Being an unusual number 16 shirt, it would originally have been prepared for European competition where more substitutes were allowed. Indeed, this style of shirt was famously worn by Celtic for the match against Ajax in the Olympic Stadium in Amsterdam on 3rd October 1971 in the first leg of the European Cup quarter-final, partnered with green shorts and yellow socks with green trim. Celtic lost this game 3-0 to the Dutch side who would go on to claim three consecutive European Cups.

This jersey style had earlier been worn as part of an all-yellow ensemble against Kokkola in the European Cup first round, first leg on 16th September 1970, to avoid a clash with the Finnish champions' green and white strip.

Unusually, Celtic also wore this shirt against Hibs in a league match on 23rd December 1972 (again with yellow shirts and socks). The normal practice at this time was for both clubs to wear their green and white home kits, although it has since become standard fare in this fixture for the away club to wear their change strip.

Celtic wore their all-yellow shirts with green shorts against Johan Cruyff's (right) Ajax in the European Cup quarter-final in 1971

HOME 1971

THE LISBON LIONS' FINAL MATCH

Match worn by Stevie Chalmers

The winds of change were blowing across Celtic Park in May 1971. The era of the Lisbon Lions was coming to an end, and construction of a brand-new main stand was already underway as the final match of season against Clyde approached.

With European Cup-winning heroes John Clark, Stevie Chalmers and Bertie Auld all set to leave the club, and the league title once more already in the bag, Jock Stein announced that the Clyde match would be the Lisbon Lions' last game. The very last time that Celtic's greatest team – Simpson, Craig, Gemmell, Murdoch, McNeill, Clark, Johnstone, Wallace, Chalmers, Auld and Lennox – would take to the pitch together.

It was a marketing masterstroke and the match drew a huge crowd, with a mighty roar greeting the players as the legendary line-up emerged – led through the construction site of the enclosure by injured goalkeeper Ronnie Simpson – and into the centre circle to take the acclaim of the crowd. Simpson was duly substituted just after the match kicked off.

In one last display of their scintillating, attacking football, Celtic destroyed their opponents in a 6-1 battering, with Bertie Auld – granted a free transfer – lifted from the pitch at the end on his team-mates' shoulders.

The jersey pictured here was worn by Lisbon match-winner Stevie Chalmers in this, his final game for Celtic, and the Celtic Park mud from that emotional day has never been washed off. After the match – in which he scored the sixth and final goal – Chalmers gave his jersey away and it only resurfaced at auction in 2008.

The short-sleeved jersey is an unusual version of the regular 'Aztec' Umbro jersey, with both the body and sleeves longer than the 1967 version and incorporating eight green hoops rather than the usual seven.

The following season was the last when the iconic, crew-necked jersey saw action. For the start of the 1972/73 season the hoops would have a new look for a new era.

Above: The Lisbon Lions wave to the enormous crowd who had come to bid their heroes farewell

Left: Injured goalkeeper Ronnie Simpson led the team out before being substituted

HOME 1972-76

Match worn from the Neilly Mochan collection

The round-collared, green-and-white-hooped jersey achieved immortality in 1967, but it had been worn as Celtic's home top as early as 1963. Almost a decade later, the 'Lisbon' strip was worn in its final competitive match in the Scottish Cup Final on 6th May 1972 – when Celtic demolished Hibs 6-1 in the 'Battle of the Greens' – and Celtic ran out for the start of the 1972/73 season in a brand-new style of shirt.

Football shirts with so-called 'v-insert' collars had been worn by the likes of Aston Villa and Tottenham Hotspur since the 1950s, but they were very much in fashion in the early 1970s as the landscape of football shirt design began to shift. Umbro had begun to sell their boxed replica kit sets – dubbed 'Umbrosets' – to great success and company rep Jim Terrace would no doubt have played a part in encouraging the club to keep up with the latest trends.

So when Celtic took to the field to face Dumbarton in the Drybrough Cup for the first match of the 1972/73 season, they did so donning this classic jersey style which epitomises 1970s Celtic. There were six green hoops and white cuffs, and they were joined by a 'floppy' collar with a white 'v' extending from the neckline into the top green hoop.

This style of jersey was worn for four seasons, perhaps most memorably during Celtic's Scottish Cup Final against Airdrieonians on 3rd May 1975. The 3-1 victory marked the end of Billy McNeill's playing career, and he was carried off the pitch on the shoulders of his team-mates. One of those team-mates – Paul Wilson – had lost his mother in the week leading up to the final. Stein had given him the option to opt out of the match, but Wilson proved the star of the show with two goals.

But the times were rapidly changing with the increasing commercialisation of football kits and the rise of the replicas market, and the Celtic jersey – virtually unchanged since the first hoops were introduced in 1903 – would inevitably be taken along for the ride.

Billy McNeill is carried off the pitch following Celtic's victory in the 1975 Scottish Cup Final

HOME 1973

Match worn from the Neilly Mochan collection

One of the rarest and most unusual of all Celtic jerseys, this version of the hoops – featuring a round-neck and collar but no 'v-insert' – was worn for just a single game.

On 8th September 1973, Celtic's players emerged from the players' tunnel wearing these one-off shirts for the first home league match of the season against near-neighbours Clyde. In fact, the difference between this style and the team's usual kit of the early 1970s was so subtle that most fans would not have noticed the change and its existence was never acknowledged in either the *Celtic View* or the matchday programme.

This one-off departure from the usual jersey occurred on a very special occasion, the day when Celtic celebrated their record-breaking eighth league title in a row. Indeed, the achievement was marked by another departure from kit tradition when, rather than their usual player numbers, each member of the team ran out onto the pitch with the No.8 on their shorts.

As part of the celebrations, Jock Stein's wife, Jean, was invited to unfurl the League Championship flag, which she did gracefully to leave eight flags flying from flagpoles above the 'Jungle' enclosure. A crowd of 25,000, cheerful in the late summer sunshine, applauded as Celtic began their quest to win a ninth title in a row with a 5-0 win.

The reason for using this one-off set of shirts remains a mystery. Neilly Mochan Junior believes that it was most likely a prototype kit sent to the club by Umbro. He explains that often these would end up in his father's storage cupboard or used in training or practice games – using one for a competitive match was pretty much unheard of.

What fate became of these 'eight-in-a-row' shirts is unknown but certainly they were never worn in a match again, and apart from this one – which was kept by Neilly Mochan – no further examples have ever surfaced. This makes it one of the rarest of all Celtic jerseys, as well as one of the most unusual.

A smiling Kenny Dalglish and his Celtic team-mates take to the field before the match against Clyde in this one-off jersey, with every player also wearing shorts with a No.8 to celebrate the club's eighth title in a row

GUARDIANS OF THE HOOPS

Playing a crucial role at the heart of the club, Celtic's kitmen have always been a rare breed who ensure every player understands the importance of the sacred green and white hoops

The job of kitman at Celtic Park has always gone far beyond washing the muddy kit and hanging up the jerseys in the dressing room. Celtic's kitmen have always been trusted members of the backroom staff, an important link between the players and the manager and key contributors to the morale of the team.

One of the secrets of Celtic's success, then, can surely be attributed to the fact that in the last 50 years this role has largely been fulfilled by just two men – both ex-players and club legends with green and white blood flowing through their veins. This continuity has ensured that generations of players have pulled on the hoops under no illusion as to the values

and traditions that must be upheld by those who wear the jersey.

Since 1997, the kitman role has been filled by John Clark, one of the legendary Lisbon Lions, and before him Neilly Mochan looked after the kit for more than 30 years. Before Mochan, the job was done by members of the bootroom staff – men like Bob Rooney, Alec Dowdells and Jimmy Gribben.

With smaller squads, less kit and no numbers on the jerseys or competition sleeve patches, the job was much simpler in those days. Indeed, up until the late 1970s the team manager would be personally responsible for ordering kit for the season.

Mochan was a star player for Celtic in the 1950s and, having only been absent for the four years that it took for him to wind down his playing career with spells at Dundee United and Raith Rovers, returned to Celtic Park as first-team trainer on 10th February 1964. Among his many roles – which included running onto the pitch with a bucket of cold water and a sponge whenever a player was injured – was organising the kit.

As Jock Stein's first-team trainer during the heyday of the 1960s and '70s, Mochan not only trained the Lisbon Lions and the 'Nine-in-a-Row' team but also brought through

Neilly Mochan – a phenomenal player, remarkable kitman and a true Celtic legend without whom this book simply would not have been possible

Bob Rooney, who worked alongside Neilly Mochan in Celtic's backroom team

"Celtic's kitmen have always been trusted members of the backroom staff, an important link between the players and the manager"

Neilly Mochan (left), Jock Stein (centre) and assistant manager Sean Fallon watch on from the sidelines during the 1967 European Cup Final in Lisbon

"With the club being run on an extremely tight budget, Mochan was fiercely protective of the kit"

numerous 'groundstaff' boys who would go on to become Celtic legends in their own right, from Tommy Burns to Charlie Nicholas and George McCluskey to Paul McStay.

"Part of the groundstaff boys' role was that they would assist the kitman," explains Mochan's son, Neilly Junior. "Some of the tasks were basic – like making sure the dirty socks weren't inside-out before they were put in the laundry – but the young guys were being taught standards and discipline, which was so important. It certainly didn't do any of the players any harm."

Mochan looked after the kit under several Celtic managers – including Stein, McNeill, David Hay and Tommy Burns – with his role becoming dedicated to the kit under McNeill in the late 1970s as the whole kit operation became a bigger and more commercialised operation.

When Mochan first took on the role of kitman, the ordering of new kit – generally two new sets of home kit per season – would have been handled by the manager. Mochan would ensure that new jerseys would go to the first team, later being handed down to the reserves and the youth team before ending up as training kit and, ultimately, cut up for rags used for cleaning the dressing rooms. With the club being run on an extremely tight budget, Mochan was fiercely protective of the kit.

"On one occasion in the late eighties," Mochan Junior says, "Andy Walker was tackled by Dundee's Jim Duffy, landing him on the red ash track that surrounded the pitch at the time. There had been heavy rain that day and Andy was saturated and covered in red ash. When he came into the dressing room at half-time, he asked for a replacement jersey, but my dad told him he wasn't playing well enough to merit a replacement top. So Andy had to take his soaking wet shirt off and place it on the radiator for 15 minutes before putting it back on for the second half.

"Then there was the time when Celtic played Orlando Lions in a friendly match in September 1988. This was part of the deal that had brought former Scotland goalie Alan Rough to Parkhead the previous month, and my dad got wind that our visitors – a small amateur club – wanted to swap jerseys at full-time. Celtic were still wearing their centenary strips at that time, which had to last them until the end of the season, some eight months later."

This posed an obvious dilemma for the kitman, who didn't want to disappoint Celtic's stateside guests. Andy Murdoch, a young Celtic goalkeeper who was part of the first-team squad that day, recalls: "We wore the centenary kit for the first half but when we got in at half-time, Neilly was holding a pile of old jerseys which he handed out to each of the players as they made their way into the changing room. These were not the old shirts that the reserves wore, they weren't even the tops that the youth team were wearing at the time – they were even older than that. They had a white v-neck with no sponsor.

Celtic sported old jerseys for the second half of their friendly against Orlando Lions in 1988 – Mochan was adamant that the players should not give away any of the club's precious centenary shirts

Neilly Mochan sorts out the players' kit behind the scenes at Celtic Park

"All the boys were looking at each other, completely bemused. Neilly just said in his Falkirk accent: 'Well what are you expecting us to do? We're not giving away the centenary jerseys.' Even the goalie top that I had to wear in the second half hardly fitted me and it was covered in stains."

Despite the 1980s being the era when football was becoming more and more commercialised, Mochan treated the kit – now supplied to the club by

Umbro as part of a more formal kit deal – as he had always done. This no doubt partly came from the top of the club, with the club's supporters referring to those running Celtic during this period as 'The Biscuit Tin Board'. The highly frugal approach to the management of the kit may also explain the difficulty in obtaining certain Celtic match worn jerseys, particularly goalkeeper shirts, from this period.

"During my time at the club, Mary Mills worked in the laundry room at Parkhead," continues Murdoch. "Whenever Mary wanted to throw any item of kit out, Neilly would stop her and tell her it just needed another wash!

"At that time, there were four goalkeepers and I remember on one occasion we all needed new gloves, so we ordered two pairs each without going through Neilly. When they arrived, he was livid. We ended up in front of the manager, Billy McNeill, and got absolutely hammered for ordering supplies without Neilly knowing about it.

"He was the same when it came to getting new boots. Neilly would inspect your boots and do absolutely everything he could to avoid giving you a new pair. He would use superglue to put the soles back on. It got to the stage where you'd almost need to rip them to bits to make them completely unserviceable. I remember Gerry Creaney coming out of Neilly's room in disbelief that he was expected to continue wearing his old boots. He went out in the next reserve game and one of them fell apart on the pitch."

"My dad didn't scrimp and save for the sake of it," confirms Mochan Junior. "It was the way the club was being run at that time. I remember when Andy Walker signed in 1987, he was handed a new pair of boots by my dad – they were adidas World Cup 1982 boots. They had been in his store cupboard, in their box, for five years. That's how Celtic did things back then. He'd always be winding the players up. He'd pick on the

Sean Fallon and Neilly Mochan (right) race from the Celtic dugout as the final whistle goes with Celtic having just clinched the 1965 Scottish Cup

strong first-teamers and stand up for the youngsters. If an experienced player wanted new boots, his favourite putdown was: 'Have you been kicking that dugout wall? You're never on the park, so the holes in your boots couldn't have come from kicking a ball.'

"It wasn't just the young boys who got that treatment," Murdoch continues. "Big Paul Elliott joined from Pisa as a big-name signing in 1989. The boots he brought over with him were the most beautiful Italian soft leather boots. Paul told his young apprentice he wasn't allowed to touch them with boot polish. He insisted that they were only treated with baby oil. Neilly went absolutely crazy. 'Baby oil? Baby oil? You don't get baby oil here, son. It's black polish or nothing.' Big Paul didn't know where to look. He thought Neilly was winding him up. Even the biggest, most expensive high-profile players were treated the same way by Neilly."

Sourcing and maintaining boots had always been part of Mochan's kitroom operation. During the 1960s Umbro were the UK's official distributor of adidas football boots and before the 1967 European Cup Final they offered Celtic a lucrative deal that would see the entire team wear the German manufacturer's boots for the Lisbon encounter with Inter Milan.

"However, some of the guys – Billy McNeill and Jim Craig, for example – wore Puma and they didn't want to wear new boots for the first time in such an important game," says Mochan Junior. "So, on the night before the match, my dad went around the players' rooms and took all the boots that weren't adidas. He then covered up the Puma logos with black polish before painting three white stripes over the top of them. If you look closely at the photo of Billy McNeill shaking hands with Inter Milan's captain, you can see that he

Billy McNeill – wearing his customised 'adidas' boots – lines up with the match officials and Inter Milan captain Armando Picchi before the 1967 European Cup Final

is wearing Puma boots with adidas stripes painted on."

By the time Fergus McCann took over Celtic in 1994, the club was being paid well to wear Umbro strips and the amount of kit available had increased dramatically. That didn't, however, mean that the floodgates in Mochan's kitroom opened.

"When Fergus McCann arrived, players were able to swap as often as they liked, but they were charged for the shirts," says Mochan Junior. "It was taken out of their wages. Andy Walker was even charged for the jersey he wore at the press conference when he re-signed for the club!"

In addition, all the shirt embroidery for one-off games, cup finals and later testimonials was organised by Mochan.

"For the Danny McGrain testimonial in 1980, he was also responsible for having the players' names added to the back of

each jersey for the first time," Mochan Junior adds. "Pat Bonner's name was spelt incorrectly and appeared as 'Bonnar'. This may have been a prank by my dad, as he used to wind 'Big Packie' up all the time and call him 'The Oracle', on account of him seemingly knowing everything about everything. In saying that, it may have been a genuine mistake, because my dad's goalie at Celtic in the 1950s was John Bonnar. Either way, Big Packie would not have been happy. If he ever asked for new gloves, my dad would respond: 'You don't need gloves to pick the ball out the back of the net, son.'"

Mochan continued as kitman into a new era of third kits and radically designed away jerseys. "He used to shake his head at some of the modern designs of the away kits," says Mochan Junior. "But he accepted that the game was changing."

When the time came to replace Mochan after he sadly passed away in 1994 – the day after Celtic first wore numbers on the back of the hoops in a league game – the baton was eventually passed on to another ex-player in Lisbon Lion John Clark, who at the

Neilly Mochan, pictured at Celtic Park in 1984

John Clark pictured celebrating with his fellow Lisbon Lions in 1967 (below) and in the Celtic kitroom in 2007 (right)

time of writing was still in the role. In the modern world of football where managers and players come and go, it represents a remarkable continuity and ensures that the traditions of the club continue to receive the respect they deserve.

In Clark's time at the club, of course, the role of kitman has changed almost beyond recognition. There are now three new kits every season, short and long-sleeved variations, base-layers, warm-up outfits, first-team squads of more than 30 players, with individual names and numbers, different sleeve patches for every competition and alternative sponsor logos for European matches. This means that what was once a part-time job for one of the club's trainers is now a full-time managerial role overseeing a whole team of kitroom staff.

Clark himself describes his job as "like running the men's department at Marks & Spencers" – albeit with far longer opening hours. "My preparations begin the day after the game before – getting the kit washed and ready, replacing shirts that have been given away or damaged. It's a seven-days-a-

week job and not for a young man with a family because it would end in divorce. I'm in at 8am and I leave when I'm finished."

Despite all the modern complications, however, Clark says that there is one part of the job that has got easier – cleaning the players' boots. "It's night-and-day from how it was in terms of weight, as the ones we wore absorbed so much water. The synthetic boots they wear now are a doddle to clean. You don't need to polish them – you just wipe them down with a damp cloth."

One thing that has not changed is the role of the kitman in keeping up the general morale of the squad and the team spirit of the dressing room. When Henrik Larsson signed for Celtic in 1997, Clark introduced himself and showed the new Swedish signing around Celtic Park. He showed Larsson pictures of Celtic's European Cup-winning team from 30 years before and, much to Larsson's amazement, Clark pointed himself out in the pictures. He couldn't believe that a European Cup winner would be looking after his kit and preparing his boots.

From that moment on, Clark and Larsson developed a strong friendship. It is a bond that continues to this day, with Larsson visiting Clark whenever he is back in Scotland. The wily kitman provided a sounding board to the popular Swede during some of his toughest times as a player – most notably when he broke his leg horrifically in 1999 – and, over pots of tea in the laundry room, ensured that the striker understood what it meant to represent this unique club in the green and white hoops.

While men like Neilly Mochan and John Clark are woven into the fabric at Parkhead and continue to pass on the club's traditions and spirit on to each new generation of players, Celtic will maintain the allure that makes it a club like no other.

CHAPTER FOUR
THE DAWNING OF A NEW ERA
UMBRO 1976-84

THE KIT REVOLUTION

The 1970s witnessed huge changes in football, and the Celtic jersey that had hardly been altered for decades underwent several significant and often controversial transformations

A
t some point during the 1960s, Celtic supporters began to chant a terrace song that includes the line, "And if you know the history." Appreciating the reason for the club's foundation and a knowledge of its illustrious past is fundamental to most followers of the team.

That is why the famous hooped jerseys – the most tangible expression of this cultural identity – are considered sacred and why for so long there was strong opposition to the addition of any adornment or embellishment whatsoever.

But as football entered the 1970s, times were changing. Having been unblemished by numbers, badges or logos for close to a century, the increasing commercialisation of football meant that the days of the untainted hoops were numbered.

The first hint of a new era for football kits was sparked by the manufacturers – most notably the English company Admiral.

As the sixties rolled into the seventies, football clubs continued to purchase their playing kit from their chosen manufacturer via a sports distributor – in Celtic's case The Sportman's Emporium in Vincent Street. However, since the relatively plain and simple jerseys that the teams wore incorporated no identifying manufacturer labels – or in Celtic's case even the team badge – there was nothing to stop rival manufacturers producing and selling identical strips. 'Celtic' jerseys were therefore being produced and sold by several manufacturers, including Admiral.

Then Admiral founder Bert Patrick realised that if he paid clubs to wear his company's kit, and made the shirt designs modern and more appealing to younger supporters, he could massively expand the replica kit market – safe in the knowledge that parents would have to buy his trademarked 'official' strips.

Having first signed up Leeds United in 1973, a year later Admiral agreed a sensational deal to supply the England national team, with the FA agreeing a contract that would see them earn a 10 per cent royalty on all shirt sales with an annual £150,000 advance.

The modern kit deal was born and the replica kit market for children – adult sizes were not produced until the early 1980s – exploded into life. By the mid 1970s Admiral were supplying numerous high-

Despite not supplying the club's playing kit, Admiral were selling their own 'Celtic' jerseys in the early 1970s

Admiral United 1973-74

"The increasing commercialisation of football meant that the days of the untainted hoops were numbered"

Above: Alfie Conn in the first Umbro-branded Celtic shirt in 1976

Above right: At first, Umbro's newly branded replica kits were squarely aimed at the junior market

profile English clubs, including Manchester United and Tottenham Hotspur, as well as Scottish teams like Aberdeen, Arbroath, Dundee, Kilmarnock and Motherwell. Club shirts that had not changed for decades were suddenly adorned with all manner of logos, stripes and trims. Most notably, they were plastered with Admiral logos.

Ever the traditionalists, the Celtic board were never likely to jump aboard the Admiral bandwagon. However, those running the club recognised the need to get a slice of the action. But if current kit suppliers Umbro were now going to have to pay for the privilege of supplying the

famous hoops, they would want something in return – the inclusion of their logo on the team jerseys at the very least. Otherwise, there would be nothing to stop other manufacturers like Admiral selling their 'Celtic' jerseys.

On 31st July 1976, then, Celtic played a pre-season friendly against Inverness Thistle in a set of short-sleeved hoops that were unchanged from the style of the previous season except for the addition of a black Umbro 'double diamond' logo. A small but significant change in the history of the Celtic jersey, but it was – of course – only the beginning.

HOME 1976/77

Match worn from the Neilly Mochan collection

The first outfield Celtic jersey to feature a manufacturer logo was released at the start of the 1976/77 season.

Although it would have been barely noticeable to most supporters, the small black Umbro 'double diamond' mark that was stamped on the left breast of the v-insert jersey style worn since 1972 represented the start of a huge period of change for the previously untarnished hoops.

When the new kit was first worn, against Inverness Thistle in a friendly on 31st July 1976, a small green Umbro logo also appeared on the shorts.

Although the exact details of Celtic's arrangement with Umbro are unknown, this landmark effectively marked the club's first modern kit deal whereby the club would receive payment (in the form of royalties on replica kits sold) for wearing the manufacturer's product, rather than purchasing it as they had done for the previous 40 years or so.

The new shirts appeared at a time of change on the pitch as well as off it, with Jock Stein returning to the dugout for the beginning of the 1976/77 season following his recuperation after a near-fatal car crash. Stein navigated Celtic to a league and Scottish Cup double. There is a firmly held belief amongst fans that had new signings Pat Stanton and Joe Craig not been cup-tied, Celtic would have added the League Cup to their trophy haul for a historic treble in their newly branded kits.

Now that manufacturer logos had been introduced to the sacred hoops, there was no going back. In little over a year, the Celtic crest would also be embroidered on the jersey. Although there would be opposition to the inclusion of a crest and sponsor in the letters pages of the *Celtic View* weekly newspaper, the addition of the Umbro logo barely raised an eyebrow and there was no negative reaction.

Kenny Dalglish and Rangers' John Greig during an Old Firm derby in the 1976/77 season. Celtic's jerseys carried Umbro branding before those of Rangers

SCOTTISH CUP FINAL 1977

Match prepared from the Damian Donald collection

To mark the occasion of the 1977 Scottish Cup Final on 7th May, the Celtic players wore jerseys incorporating match-detail embroidery for the first time.

Unusually, this embroidery – as well as the heat-pressed Umbro logo – appeared in bright red. Since the showpiece occasion was due to be televised live for the first time in 55 years, it is likely that Umbro selected red for their logo to make it more visible to television viewers and the match detail was stitched to match.

When the Celtic players took to the Hampden Park pitch for the final against Rangers, they did so wearing smart white tracksuit tops with 'League Champions 1977' stitched onto the back in large green lettering.

By the end of the game Celtic were the league and Scottish Cup double winners by virtue of an Andy Lynch penalty after 20 minutes. All the players were allowed to keep their match jerseys and Lynch still has his, framed and mounted on the wall of his office, as it marks the high point of his playing career.

The late Paul Wilson (who passed away in the 40th anniversary year of this triumph) also had his jersey framed and mounted at his home. Wilson curiously took to the field wearing shorts adorned with No.14, even though he started the game.

The featured jersey belonged to assistant manager Davie McParland, but was later sold at auction.

Kenny Dalglish played his last competitive game for Celtic in this final, although he lost his winners medal during the on-field celebrations. Thankfully, a policeman later retrieved the medal from a disabled fan's umbrella at the side of the Hampden pitch.

The match is also notable for being the last time Jock Stein won a trophy with the club.

Above: Danny McGrain celebrates with Alfie Conn in their match-embroidered shirts

Left: Kitman Neilly Mochan arranged for the 'League Champions 1977' message to be stitched onto the back of the players' tracksuit tops

HOME 1977-79

Match worn from the Neilly Mochan collection

Apart from the very first all-white jersey last worn in 1889, unlike nearly every other major football team the Celtic jersey had never included the club badge. The famous hoops, it was felt, were enough to convey the club's identity. But all that changed in the summer of 1977 when the new home shirt was revealed.

Although the style of the jersey remained unchanged from the design first introduced in 1972, the hoops unveiled before the 1977/78 season featured the club's four-leaf clover badge – which had been in use since the 1930s – boldly embroidered in the centre of the shirt.

The arrival of the club crest was inevitable. If Umbro were to be able to maximise the sales of replica kits – aimed at the junior market and available in box sets – it was crucial that their strips were easily identifiable as the official kit.

The decision was not universally popular, however. Many supporters penned their grievances to the club's official weekly newspaper, the *Celtic View*, with one letter angrily insisting, "You don't need a badge on the jersey, everybody knows it's Celtic."

Another more subtle development on the new jersey was the introduction of the word 'Umbro' beneath the company's logo, which now appeared in white.

The new jersey was first worn on 13th August 1977 – the day that the club unfurled Jock Stein's last League Championship flag – in the season opener against Dundee United. Although the campaign that followed was trophyless and spelled the end of Stein's reign, the jersey was retained for the historic 1978/79 season under Billy McNeill.

Celtic went into their last league game of McNeill's debut season on Monday 21st May 1979 requiring a win against Rangers to reclaim the title. Rangers still had two games in hand and only needed a point to keep their championship hopes alive. With Rangers a goal up, Celtic's firebrand winger Johnny Doyle was sent off after 51 minutes. In true Celtic style, however, McNeill's men rallied and went on to win 4-2 in dramatic fashion on the night when 'Ten Men Won the League'.

Above: Alfie Conn gets a shot away against Clyde in August 1978

Right: The long-sleeved version of this classic version of the hoops

Far right: In 1975, Celtic began wearing numbers on their shirts for European matches, so this No.8 jersey would have been worn in European Cup games

AWAY 1977/78

Player shirt from the Neilly Mochan collection

Another all-yellow change kit was introduced in 1977, seven years on from the first Celtic strip to use this colour scheme.

This jersey is notable for being the first away shirt style to incorporate Celtic's four-leaf clover crest, which was placed in the centre of the jersey in the same position as on the home kit. The design was virtually identical to the favoured goalkeeper jersey of the time. However, the outfield players only ever wore the short-sleeved version in a competitive match – unusually with red numbers – with the goalkeeper switching to green on these occasions.

This style of yellow jersey was first worn at Celtic Park in the European Cup first round first leg match against Luxembourg champions Jeunesse d'Esch on 14th September 1977. Celtic comfortably swept the part-timers aside 5-0, with goals from Roddie MacDonald, Paul Wilson, Joe Craig (two) and Brian McLaughlin.

It was worn twice further that month, against Clydebank in a 1-0 league win, and in the return European match against Jeunesse, which Celtic won 6-1. The stylish kit made another appearance in the second round of the European Cup against SSW Innsbruck on 2nd November 1977. In the second leg in Austria (and with Celtic defending a 2-1 lead), Jock Stein's side capitulated and lost three goals in under half-an-hour. This was enough to eliminate Celtic from the competition in what was to be Stein's last European match in charge of the club.

For the remainder of the 1977/78 season, Celtic wore older change kits instead of this all-yellow outfit, which meant reappearances for the yellow jersey with green collar and the all-green round-neck shirt, which hadn't been seen since 1973.

The jersey featured here, which was sourced from Neilly Mochan's collection, has no number on the back and is therefore likely to have been a spare which was never match worn – either as an outfield or goalkeeper jersey.

Celtic were all smiles as they easily put part-timers Jeunesse d'Esch to the sword in the European Cup

AWAY 1978-80

Player shirt from the Joe Arcari collection

Celtic's all-green away kit, launched before Billy McNeill's first season in charge, harked back to the bottle-green change jerseys of the new manager's playing days. However, with its modern Umbro branding and shiny polyester look, it also represented a dramatic step into the future of the Celtic jersey.

The most notable feature of what has become a cult classic jersey design – and a holy grail for Celtic match worn shirt collectors – is the distinctive Umbro-branded taping down the sleeves. This fondly remembered feature of Umbro jerseys of the late 1970s was a response to the early Admiral kits which so revolutionised football shirt design with their sleeve stripes containing multiple manufacturer logos. The 'double diamond' pattern also featured (in green) down the side of the white shorts and around the tops of the green socks.

On the jersey pictured, two large Umbro logos are positioned on the large white wing collar. However, other variations had no logos on the collar and a more traditional logo – with Umbro lettering below – on the left breast.

Although first worn on 21st October 1978 in a scoreless league stalemate against Morton, this jersey is most famous for its appearance in the Bernabeu on 19th March 1980 for the second leg of the European Cup quarter-final against Real Madrid. Celtic went into this encounter with a two-goal cushion thanks to goals from George McCluskey and Johnny Doyle, but lost 3-0 in Spain to go crashing out of the competition.

With Real Madrid in their traditional all-white, Celtic wore green shorts for this match. The game was played on a warm evening in the Spanish capital and all the Celtic players wore short sleeves, with many of them changing into fresh jerseys at half-time. This means that a combination of the two variations of the jersey were worn in the same match.

Above: Goalkeeper Peter Latchford (right) puts a comforting arm around Bobby Lennox following Celtic's 3-0 defeat at the Bernabeu

Right: The No.6 applied to this jersey is not in the usual font seen on this shirt style and may have been applied later

HOME 1979-82

Match worn from the Neilly Mochan collection

The classic v-necked version of the hoops worn between 1979 and 1982 is one of the most popular incarnations of the Celtic jersey.

Celtic actually began the 1979/80 season wearing the so-called 'Ten Men Won the League' jersey from the previous season. However, on 27th October they unveiled this new design for the 1-0 win against Rangers.

Apart from the stylish, bold white v-neck collar, the other most notable difference was the positioning of the club crest. An early prototype of the jersey – a photograph of which had appeared in the *Celtic View* – had the badge in the centre of the jersey. However, when it was finally worn in anger the club crest had moved to the more traditional position above the left breast with the white embroidered Umbro logo now located above the right breast.

During the course of its three-season lifespan, two variations of this jersey were worn. There was a cotton version, as per the example pictured here and a shiny polyester alternative. This was an era when developments in fabric manufacturing were rapidly advancing and lightweight polyester shirts with reflective shadow stripes and other patterns within the material would soon become the norm.

The jersey featured here includes a black number and would therefore have been prepared for European competition by kitman Neilly Mochan.

This shirt's most celebrated appearance was against Real Madrid in the European Cup quarter-final first leg at Celtic Park on 5th March 1980. On a memorable night, Celtic scored two second-half goals through George McCluskey and Johnny Doyle to sensationally beat the Spaniards 2-0. Although Celtic would succumb to a 3-0 reverse in the Bernabeu in the second leg, the Parkhead victory is still regarded as a classic European night at Celtic Park.

Tommy Burns in action during Celtic's pre-season match against St Mirren on 8th August 1981

SCOTTISH CUP FINAL 1980

Match worn from the Neilly Mochan collection

The Celtic jersey worn in the 1980 Scottish Cup Final against Rangers is an adapted version of the home shirt the club had worn all season, which is ranked among collectors as one of the finest examples of the eighties.

The cotton jersey, with embroidered Umbro logo, was specially adapted for the occasion with match-specific embroidery, which was the responsibility of kitman Neilly Mochan. Mochan utilised the services of local companies for such tasks and would often send a member of the Parkhead groundstaff to pick up the match-prepared jerseys when they were ready.

Celtic won the match by a single goal after extra-time thanks to George McCluskey, who diverted a hopeful shot by Danny McGrain past the wrong-footed Rangers' goalkeeper, Peter McCloy. Sadly, the match was not remembered for a Celtic triumph; instead, it is renowned as 'The Second Hampden Riot'. This unenviable title was bestowed on the occasion due to the violent after-match scenes inside the stadium, reminiscent of the 1909 disorder that also followed an Old Firm Scottish Cup Final.

After snatching the win late in the game, the Celtic players celebrated in front of their supporters. The 10-foot-high perimeter fences were scaled by over-zealous Hoops fans eager to join their heroes on the pitch. The Rangers fans invaded the pitch and charged the Celtic contingent, who in turn confronted their aggressors. What ensued was an on-pitch riot.

The incident resulted in both clubs being fined £20,000, while George Younger, Scotland's Secretary of State, blamed the riotous scenes on the sale and consumption of alcohol as well as the initial actions of the Celtic supporters. An act of parliament was later passed banning the sale of alcoholic beverages within Scottish sports grounds.

Tommy Burns leaves Rangers' Bobby Russell trailing in his wake as Celtic battle their way to a 1-0 cup final victory that would be sadly tarnished by crowd trouble

CUP FINAL TRACKSUITS

The occasion of a cup final has come to require a club suit, embroidered jersey and cup final tracksuit. Some of these classic tracksuit examples are so timeless that they have been reproduced in recent years for the modern fan. They were normally worn on cup final day for the pre-match pleasantries with the chosen dignitaries, kept on during a quick warm-up on the Hampden pitch, and then handed to kitman Neilly Mochan – who invariably stored them in one of his kit hampers for years to come.

SCOTTISH CUP FINAL 1973

v Rangers, Hampden Park

LEAGUE CUP FINAL 1977/78

v Rangers, Hampden Park

SCOTTISH CUP FINAL 1980

v Rangers, Hampden Park

LEAGUE CUP FINAL 1983/84

v Rangers, Hampden Park

SCOTTISH CUP FINAL 1984

v Aberdeen, Hampden Park

SCOTTISH CUP FINAL 1985

v Dundee United, Hampden Park

SCOTTISH CUP FINAL 1990

v Aberdeen, Hampden Park

AWAY 1981-83

Player shirt from the Neilly Mochan collection

In the summer of 1981, Celtic introduced two new change jerseys – green with white pinstripes and white with green pinstripes – making 1981/82 the first season when the club had three recognised kits.

The v-necked polyester shirts were from an Umbro template that was used by a number of British clubs (including Rangers) in the early eighties. The fact that all three kits were green and white, and therefore offered very little as a practical alternative to the hoops, is a clear indication that these releases were squarely aimed at the growing replica shirt market rather than to help avoid colour clashes.

Although it was never specifically named as the 'away' jersey, the green shirt certainly got more outings than its white counterpart, which is therefore generally considered to have been the club's 'third' alternative.

The green jersey was generally worn with white shorts and green socks, although when Celtic wore it for the first time – against Juventus in the 2-0 European Cup first round second leg defeat on 30th September 1981 – they played in all-green.

Nearly a year to the day later, the green jersey attained cult status when it was worn in a classic European Cup encounter against Ajax. Having drawn the home leg 2-2, Charlie Nicholas put Celtic ahead after 35 minutes in Amsterdam when he chipped Hans Galjé following a delicate pass from Frank McGarvey. Ajax equalised half-an-hour later to put them ahead on away goals, but with two minutes remaining substitute George McCluskey scored the winner.

Afterwards, Celtic's match-winning hero visited the Ajax changing room where he found Netherlands and Ajax legend Johan Cruyff – cigarette in mouth – and swapped jerseys.

Largely due to the memory of that famous triumph, the simple pinstripe design was and remains a hugely popular style, with New Balance producing a near carbon-copy for the 2015/16 season.

Davie Provan on the ball during Celtic's 5-0 demolition of Kilmarnock in April 1983

THIRD 1981-83

Player shirt from the Neilly Mochan collection

The white with green pinstripes 'third' jersey was not worn nearly as often as the green 'away' version. In fact, it wasn't worn at all during the 1981/82 season.

Celtic's colours traditionally clashed with sides such as Airdrieonians, Clydebank, Ayr United, Kilmarnock and St Mirren, whose home jerseys contained a significant element of white. That meant that on the occasions when Celtic needed a change of kit they generally selected to wear the green version.

Even when facing Hibernian, both clubs still traditionally wore their home kits in 'The Battle of the Greens' – as Jock Stein once called it – and this remained the case during Easter Road clashes between the two sides during the 1981/82 campaign. On 27th November 1982, however, Celtic ran out at Easter Road for the league match against Hibs wearing their white 'third' kit for the very first time.

It proved a lucky choice as Celtic won 3-2 with two goals from Frank McGarvey and one from a young Paul McStay. The 'lucky' white jerseys were worn again for the second league encounter at Easter Road in April 1983, this time in a 3-0 win. However, Celtic reverted to the traditional hoops for both visits to Leith during the following season.

Whilst the green away kit went on to secure something of an iconic status, due in large part to the huge European nights on which it was worn, the white alternative – worn with green shorts and white socks – has become a cult classic. Having been used on so few occasions, match worn examples are extremely rare and even original replicas have become something of a collector's item.

The example featured on these pages comes from Neilly Mochan's collection. It has no green number on the back and, therefore, is not match worn. It is, however, the only known surviving example of a player-issued jersey in this style, making it one of the rarest jerseys in this book.

Tommy Burns is pictured in this rare white jersey during the 3-0 victory over Hibs at Easter Road in April 1983

HOME 1982-84

Match worn from the Neilly Mochan collection

The new home jersey released in time for the 1982/83 season featured the addition of pinstripes above and below each of the six hoops. Subtle it may have been, but this represented the most radical adaptation of Celtic's sacred shirt design in nearly 100 years.

In addition to the horizontal pinstripes, the v-necked collar now incorporated a thick green line which was matched on the cuffs. The design was still classical enough to please the traditionalists and the new version of the hoops was accepted by fans without complaint.

First worn in the early season League Cup sectional matches, this kit included the white shorts and socks from the previous season. The European variation of this jersey carried the now obligatory black numbers on the back and it was worn against Ajax and Real Sociedad in 1982, Aarhus, Sporting Lisbon and Nottingham Forest in 1983, and Gent in 1984.

When Ajax arrived in Glasgow for the first of these European encounters, Celtic offered them the use of their Barrowfield training ground. After training at the dilapidated 'complex', the Dutch staff were convinced that they had been tricked and refused to believe that Barrowfield could possibly be where Celtic practised.

After the match – in which the Ajax side (which included Jan Molby, Johan Cruyff and Jesper Olsen, with Marco van Basten and Frank Rijkaard on the bench) played in blue – the away team's kitman discovered that the kit hamper had gone missing as they were loading the team bus. In a panic, he raced onto the bus and ordered the players to help him find it. Off trooped Molby, van Basten, Rijkaard et al (Cruyff remained on the bus smoking a cigarette) and they paired up to knock on the doors of Parkhead tenement buildings looking for their stolen gear.

The strips were never seen again…

Murdo MacLeod plays the ball in the hoops, now with the addition of horizontal pinstripes

AWAY 1983/84

Match worn by Jim Melrose and Brian McClair

Celtic's popular pinstripe change kits were replaced by yet another stylish Umbro jersey in 1983 – the manufacturer was on a good run of form when it came to designing the Glasgow side's away strips.

The introduction of lime green was an inspired choice, and it is a colour that the club has returned to sporadically – with mixed results – in later years. This early example, however, seemed to garner unanimous praise amongst Celtic supporters from the moment it was released.

The cuffs and collar of this jersey were the same green tone as the previous season's white with green pinstripes change kit, but two white stripes were added in a subtle design change. The four-leaf clover crest was again boldly embroidered on the left breast, and the Umbro emblem with lowercase lettering was stitched to the right breast in black.

The main body of this jersey was simply lime green with no additional detail, and it worked perfectly. The kit was finished off with green shorts and socks that matched the jersey's collar and cuff colour scheme.

Most fondly remembered for its appearances in European competitions, this strip was first worn in the UEFA Cup first round second leg tie against Aarhus in Denmark on 28th September 1983 (a match won 4-1 with goals from Murdo MacLeod, Frank McGarvey, Roy Aitken and Davie Provan).

A more memorable outing than the jersey's debut undoubtedly took place in the following round of the UEFA Cup against Sporting Lisbon on 2nd November 1983. With Celtic 2-0 down from the first leg, the lime green jersey was worn at Parkhead as the home side produced a memorable 5-0 victory to win the tie.

The No.11 shirt featured here would have been worn by Jim Melrose (against Aarhus) and Brian McClair (versus Sporting Lisbon), as kitman Neilly Mochan was only supplied with two sets of jerseys (long and short-sleeved) for the entire season.

Brian McClair – with Frank McGarvey, Paul McStay and Davie Provan – celebrates scoring against Sporting Lisbon at Celtic Park

PROTOTYPES

UMBRO 1981

Before a new design of jersey is adopted, kit manufacturers will produce prototypes to present to the club. Some examples of shirt designs that never made it into the Celtic Park kitroom have made their way into the hands of collectors.

In 1981 Umbro produced a version of the new home jersey with the club crest located in the centre of the chest, as it had been on the previous version of the hoops.

This jersey actually appeared in a photograph in the *Celtic View* alongside the new green and white pinstriped away and third kits. However, by the time the season kicked off the badge had been moved to the left breast, where it has pretty much remained ever since.

There are two known examples of this prototype jersey in the hands of collectors, including the one pictured here.

GOLA 1990s

In the early nineties, Gola made a bid
to secure Celtic's kit manufacturing and
shirt sponsorship deals, which resulted
in a number of prototype designs being
presented to the club.

Incredibly, one such jersey design
replaced the famous green and white
hoops with a geometric pattern of green
and black-outlined white diamonds.
Thankfully the club knocked back this
sacrilegious notion.

Later in the 1990s, the jersey that Celtic
wore to stop Rangers from winning 10
league titles in succession in 1997/98
originally had the CR Smith logo across
the front of the shirt. This design appeared
in an Umbro advert in popular weekly
magazine *Shoot!* However, negotiations
between the club and the glazing firm
broke down and the jersey ended up with
a large Umbro logo on the front instead.

KEEPING THE FAITH

The guardians of the Celtic goal have included some true club legends and their match worn jerseys are amongst the rarest of all

In the earliest days of football, little thought was given to the shirt worn by a side's goalkeeper. Indeed, until the International Football Association Board instituted a rule change in 1909, goalkeepers had by and large worn the same strip as outfield players.

Following this change, Celtic usually opted for either red, green or yellow jerseys for their goalkeepers right up to the mid-eighties, when a grey goalie top was introduced for the first time and worn with distinction by Pat Bonner.

John Thomson was wearing red the final time he graced the pitch during a match at Ibrox on 5th September 1931, when Rangers' striker Sam English accidentally collided with Celtic's young goalkeeper, who later passed away as a result of the head injury he sustained; Ronnie Simpson's 1967 European Cup Final shirt was all-green, and the 36-year-old was often seen sporting such a jersey or a yellow alternative throughout his seven years as Celtic's No.1; while Craig Gordon's treble-clinching jersey was luminous yellow in 2017.

Other colours have appeared on Celtic goalie kits, such as purple, black and pink, but arguably the most unusual goalkeeper jersey was worn during Celtic's 1912 Scandinavian tour. While in Denmark and Norway to play five friendly matches, Celtic keeper John Mulrooney appeared wearing what looked like a white knitted jersey with a series of small shamrocks making up the hoops. This creation had been gifted to the hero of the 1904 Scottish Cup Final, Jimmy Quinn, who passed it on to Mulrooney – it remains one of the most bizarre and intriguing Celtic jerseys ever worn.

The search for match worn examples of goalie jerseys for this collection has been a challenging one. Many ex-Celtic keepers from the 1950s through to the 1990s have explained how their jerseys were handed down to the reserves, then the youth team, and were then worn in training. The fact that the shot-stoppers have their own bespoke outfit also means that there were only ever a handful used every season, which has led to a dearth of Celtic goalie kits being available to collectors to date. Here is a selection of tops that the aficionados have been able to dig out from the depths of time…

During the 1912 tour of Scandinavia, Celtic goalkeeper John Mulrooney wore this 'unique' hand-knitted jersey

"The search for match worn examples of goalie tops for this collection has been a challenging one"

SCOTTISH LEAGUE CUP FINAL 1978

Match worn by Peter Latchford

When Celtic reached the League Cup Final of 1978 against Rangers, a decision had to be made on which goalkeeper would be granted permission to wear their first-choice goalkeeper jersey, as both clubs' keepers typically wore yellow. Rangers won the toss, and Peter Latchford appeared for the final in this one-off cup final goalkeeper shirt.

It will not bring back happy memories for Latchford, who fluffed an extra-time clearance onto the head of Rangers' Gordon Smith for the winning goal.

1980 DANNY McGRAIN TESTIMONIAL

Match worn by Pat Bonner

Pat 'Packie' Bonner may have gone on to make 641 competitive appearances for Celtic, winning nine domestic trophies and 80 caps for the Republic of Ireland (who he represented at two World Cups and one European Championship), but on 4th August 1980, many were still asking, "Pat who?"

Bonner had only made four appearances for Celtic, with the last one coming over a year earlier against Rangers in the Glasgow Cup Final on 16th May 1979, so he was a somewhat unfamiliar name to fans and reporters alike. So much so, that his surname was spelt incorrectly as 'Bonnar' on the back of his jersey for this match to celebrate Danny McGrain's services to Celtic.

A renowned joker, Neilly Mochan had once laid out a jersey for Bonner that had been pulled out of one of his famous kitroom stashes. The goalie top had belonged to Neilly's ex-teammate John Bonnar, who played in the 1950s. So, the question remains, was the misspelling of Bonner's name for the Danny McGrain testimonial a genuine error at the printers or a wind-up? Either way, every newspaper report followed suit the following day when describing how well the young Irishman had performed during the scoreless draw with Manchester United, with the *Daily Record's* headline reading, 'Bonnar's Bouquet! 'Keeper Saves Danny's Day.'

Pat 'Packie' Bonner (not Bonnar!) – an all-time Celtic great who wore a dizzying array of goalkeeper jersey styles

1981/82 JERSEY

Match worn by Pat Bonner

By the 1981/82 season, Pat Bonner was well-established between the sticks for Celtic. The only two games he missed throughout this campaign were two Glasgow Cup ties, and he was instrumental in Billy McNeill's side's march to the league title.

There were two alternative goalkeeper jerseys around about this time. Both had a black collar, cuffs, and underarm panels, with the body of one being yellow and the other green. The yellow top was worn far more often, but an alternative green edition was required due to Rangers having the same yellow Umbro goalie shirt.

1983/84 LEAGUE CUP FINAL

Match prepared for Pat Bonner

Celtic faced Rangers on 25th March 1984 in the first Scottish League Cup Final to be played on a Sunday, with Rangers ultimately securing a 3-2 victory.

Both sides' kits were manufactured by Umbro at this time, and the jersey shown here was meant to be the one worn in the final by Pat Bonner. However, it was the same colour and a similar design as the one used by Rangers goalie Peter McCloy and a coin toss was required to decide who wore the yellow jersey with black arms. Celtic lost the toss, which meant this featured jersey was never worn. Bonner instead wore an all-yellow jersey with no cup final embroidery.

1989-91 JERSEY

Match worn by Pat Bonner

Pat Bonner was the only ever-present during Celtic's disappointing 1989/90 season, in which the club were beaten in both cups by Aberdeen (League Cup semi-final and Scottish Cup Final), finished fifth in the league (thus failing to qualify for a European place) and lasted one round of the European Cup Winners' Cup.

This jersey was well-worn by Bonner during this grim period, and it has clearly been laundered numerous times going by the faded appearance of the sponsor and number. These tops were padded on the shoulders and elbows, and they would have been handed down through the reserve and youth sides before being used as training gear.

There was also an alternative jersey worn throughout 1989-91 which was the same design in grey and black.

1996-98 JERSEY

Match worn by Gordon Marshall

Umbro produced a plethora of 'loud' Celtic goalkeeper tops throughout the nineties. This green, black and yellow effort included the crest in a shield, as seen on the 'Bumblebee' away jersey of the era. This shirt first appeared during Tommy Burns' final campaign in charge and was worn during the ultimately fruitless 1996/97 season with the CR Smith logo across the chest (*right*).

By the time Wim Jansen replaced Burns for his sole season in charge (1997/98) the sponsor's logo was replaced with Umbro (in white). Jansen selected Gordon Marshall as his No.1 for the first three competitive matches (twice against Inter Cable-Tel in the UEFA Cup and for the league opener against Hibs), but Jonathan Gould played every other game during this double-winning season.

TOM BOYD TESTIMONIAL 2001

Match worn by Jonathan Gould

Before being replaced by Dmitri Kharine, Rab Douglas played in goal for the first half-hour of Tom Boyd's testimonial against Manchester United on 15th May 2001. This was the first time in seven attempts that Alex Ferguson was able to overcome Celtic since taking over at Old Trafford in 1986, and the 2-0 win was achieved with goals from Frenchman Mikaël Silvestre and promising teenager Bojan Djordjic.

This goalkeeper jersey was mainly black with a round-neck, which gave it the look of a similar training top that Celtic wore around the same time. The match embroidery appeared in white under the crest to match the Umbro and NTL sponsor logos. This was worn by Jonathan Gould, who was the third goalkeeper on the night.

Signed from Bradford where he had been languishing in the reserves, Jonathan Gould gave outstanding service to Celtic between 1997 and 2003

2010/11 JERSEY

Match worn by Fraser Forster

In the league match against Hibs on 6th April 2011, Celtic wore Japanese script on the back of their jerseys in memory of all those who died in the Great Tohoku Earthquake of 11th March 2011. Celtic won 3-1 against their visitors from Leith to go two points ahead of Rangers. A scoreless draw at Ibrox and a 3-2 defeat at Inverness were the two results that lost Neil Lennon the title, however, and he had to be content with a Scottish Cup win in his first full season in charge.

This grey goalie jersey was worn by Fraser Forster during the Hibs victory, and it was auctioned off along with all the other unique Celtic tops that were worn that day in an effort to raise some funds for the Japanese disaster fund.

2011/12 JERSEY

Match worn by Fraser Forster

Fraser Forster had never played a competitive match for his parent club, Newcastle United, when he saved a penalty for Celtic against Hearts on 10th December 2011. He was in the second year of his loan deal at Parkhead when he secured a vital 1-0 win by stopping Eggert Jónsson's last-minute spot-kick. Forster went on to earn a permanent move to Glasgow before returning to England's Premier League after a £10 million move to Southampton. He was welcomed at St Mary's Stadium by former team-mate Victor Wanyama, who scored Celtic's winner that day against Hearts.

Forster is a giant of a goalie, standing at 6ft 7ins. This match worn jersey from the aforementioned Hearts match is suitably large and is a stylish black design with a neon green/yellow pattern under the arms.

2013/14 AWAY JERSEY

Match worn by Fraser Forster

Celtic faced German side Greuther Fürth in a pre-season friendly ahead of the 2013/14 campaign, which ended in an embarrassing 6-2 defeat for Neil Lennon's men. Although they went on to win the championship for the third consecutive year, the Hoops endured some heavy Champions League defeats and were also eliminated from the League Cup to Championship strugglers Greenock Morton. Despite these obvious disappointments, it still came as a surprise when Lennon resigned 11 days after being presented with the League Championship trophy.

This stylish goalie jersey was worn by Fraser Forster during the defeat to the German side. The all-yellow design was classed as the 'away' jersey, with the grey version more commonly used.

2016/17 LEAGUE CUP FINAL

Match prepared for Dorus de Vries

Celtic won their 100th major trophy when they overcame Aberdeen at Hampden Park on 27th November 2016. Tom Rogic, James Forrest and Moussa Dembele got the goals as Celtic won 3-0 to give Brendan Rodgers the first part of a historic, invincible treble.

Dorus de Vries sat on the bench as the unused substitute and this yellow New Balance goalie jersey has been signed by the veteran keeper.

2017/18 LEAGUE CUP FINAL

Match prepared for Conor Hazard

Celtic wrapped up their fourth domestic honour in a row as Brendan Rodgers became the first manager in Scottish football to achieve such a feat since Jock Stein. As they had done in the previous year's final against Aberdeen, James Forrest and Moussa Dembélé got on the scoresheet to give Celtic a thoroughly deserved 2-0 win against Motherwell.

This jersey was prepared for Conor Hazard, although the young Irish goalkeeper did not make the final matchday squad.

CHAPTER FIVE
MOVING WITH THE TIMES
UMBRO 1984-93

THE ARRIVAL OF SPONSORSHIP

Far more controversial than the addition of manufacturer logos was the introduction of sponsorship to the Celtic jersey in the early 1980s

Celtic chairman Desmond White and his Rangers counterpart, John Paton, are pictured in their club's prototype CR Smith jerseys at the launch of the double sponsorship deal in September 1984

When Danish amateurs Boldklubben 1903 were drawn against Jock Stein's Celtic in the first round of the 1971/72 European Cup, their black and white jerseys incorporated the logo of local salty liquorice brand 'Delfol' across their chests. This was a highly unusual sight at the time, and it wasn't until 1977 that Hibernian became the first Scottish football club with a shirt sponsor when they signed a deal to carry the logo of sportswear brand Bukta on their jerseys.

However, this immediately caused a dispute with the television broadcasters who refused to televise Hibs matches if the club wore their sponsored jerseys. Hibs had to agree to wear unsponsored kit in televised matches to settle the row.

A full seven years later, in September 1984 – and with an agreement with the television companies to allow shirt advertising now in place – Celtic entered into their first shirt sponsorship agreement when they signed a three-year deal with Fife-based double-glazing firm CR Smith worth £250,000. The arrangement, which would see both Celtic and Rangers shirts carry the company name, was described by the *Celtic View* as: "The biggest sponsorship package in Scottish sport."

CR Smith's managing director, Gerard Eadie, had made an astute business decision to sponsor both sides of the Old Firm, thus ensuring that neither side of the city were alienated. It was a bold move by the Fife entrepreneur, who had built CR Smith into the biggest double-glazing firm in Britain at that time.

As if the joint Old Firm deal and the addition of a commercial sponsor on the front of the sacred hoops wasn't controversial enough, when the first photographs of the new sponsored jersey were published the CR Smith logo was printed in blue. Celtic's commercial director, Jack McGinn, was immediately forced onto the back foot.

"A picture of a Celtic jersey bearing the words [CR Smith] in blue appeared in

"Celtic entered into their first shirt sponsorship agreement when they signed a three-year deal with Fife-based double-glazing firm CR Smith worth £250,000"

a daily newspaper last week," he wrote in the *Celtic View*. "This was only a makeshift arrangement using a car sticker to give an impression of how the strip will look. There was never any possibility of the writing being in any colour other than black. The choice of black is to give the sponsors the maximum effect in newspaper photographs and on television."

By the time the first sponsored version of the hoops was worn in action – against Dundee at Dens Park on 29th September 1984 – the CR Smith lettering had indeed changed to black and appeared (further up the jersey than it had on the prototype) on a white patch over a green hoop.

The debut of the sponsored shirts was met with outrage on the letters page of the *Celtic View*, with George and Annie Dailly, from Kilsyth, insisting that the sponsor was "an insult to the Celtic jersey".

"We were at Celtic Park on Saturday, 15th September 1984 to say goodbye to a lifetime's love," their letter stated. "We feel we cannot watch Celtic players in a jersey that bears the name of any sponsor."

In reply, the *Celtic View* editor made a valiant attempt to explain the club's position.

"It is an unpleasant fact that Celtic cannot now operate on turnstile money alone, in common with all big clubs in Britain," he wrote. "Another unpleasant fact is that people don't turn out as readily to watch reserves matches as they used to, in fact the average attendance at reserves games is only in the hundreds, so it is hard to imagine

Frank McGarvey, Davie Provan and Roy Aitken celebrate after beating Dundee United in the 1985 Scottish FA Cup Final, the first final Celtic played with a sponsor's logo on the hoops

By the time of Celtic's centenary in 1988, the replica kit market for adults was booming

an injection of cash from this avenue.

"Lastly, most Celtic fans down through the years have a tremendous affection for the hooped jersey but they show their loyalty through following the team even when they don't agree with policy decisions or team selections or other matters surrounding the team."

Slowly but surely, Celtic supporters became used to having CR Smith on the front of the hoops as well as a variety of increasingly off-the-wall away jerseys as Umbro fully embraced the expanding replica kit market, which by now was squarely aimed at adult supporters who wanted to show their colours.

The first arrangement with CR Smith came to an end in 1991 (it would be resurrected two years later), giving way to a new commercial relationship which spawned probably the most controversial Celtic jersey in the club's history.

For one season only – 1991/92 – Celtic were sponsored by Peoples Ford, whose logo just happens to be red and blue. It seems incredible now that this was allowed to happen. Brian Gilda, the car showroom company's chairman and managing director as well as a lifelong Celtic fan, picks up the story.

"I was contacted by Terry Cassidy [Celtic's then chief executive] who offered me the opportunity to have Peoples Ford

on the Celtic jerseys for at least a season," he said. "I was wary of having the company name on just the Celtic shirt, as it could end up alienating the other side of the city. But of course my Celtic DNA then took over and we went for it, even though I thought the deal might get me into bother somewhere along the line.

"Television advertising is very expensive, so having Peoples Ford on the Celtic shirts guaranteed that the business was going to be in a lot of living rooms every weekend.

"My company name is actually Peoples, not Peoples Ford, but the brand I am associated with most is Ford so I really wanted to make sure the Ford part was included. Under normal circumstances I would have gone to Ford and asked permission because they are very protective of their brand, but this would have delayed matters so I decided just to go with it, deal with any fallout and apologise later.

With its wacky design and red and blue sponsor's logo, Celtic's 1991/92 away shirt is arguably the club's most controversial jersey

John Collins and Paul McStay, with manager Liam Brady, model the 1991/92 hoops complete with the Peoples Ford logo which outraged many fans

would be equally split between Celtic fans and Rangers fans. The immediate response I remember from the Celtic fans was, 'How can you put blue on a Celtic shirt?' Alongside the blue of the Ford logo, the Peoples lettering was red, but it came out looking orange on the jerseys, and this upset the Celtic supporters further. Then the Rangers fans were unhappy with where our money was going. In the early days, some people refused to buy cars from us because we sponsored Celtic. It really got quite nasty.

"When I look back at that time, the club were in dire straits and they didn't have enough funds to compete. You would think that it was the worst time possible to have the company name on the jersey, but the awareness of Peoples went through the roof. Everybody had a view on us.

"The sponsorship has left a legacy of sorts. A pal of mine was at a Simple Minds concert somewhere in Europe a few years ago, and there in the front row was someone with a Peoples Ford Celtic away shirt on. At first, that strip was voted one of the worst kits ever, but it is now viewed as one of the most iconic strips of all time. I'm not too sure how that happened!

"Despite my early concerns, the whole thing seemed to completely pass Ford by. They are an American company, so the fact that their logo was on Celtic's shirts went right over their heads.

"Sponsoring the Celtic jersey was certainly one of those decisions which was of the moment. Would I do it again? I don't know to be honest with you. Having said all that, it was a terrific time."

"We agreed on the home jersey, which was a simple set of hoops with Peoples Ford across the middle. But then I was shown the away strip, which bamboozled me when I first saw it. The patterned design reminded me of a stock market graph, but I trusted that Umbro were experts in their field and they understood the market, so I didn't want to tinker too much with what they were doing. Then the furore broke… all over the place!

"At that time, Peoples Ford had businesses in Glasgow, Falkirk, Livingston and Liverpool, and our Scottish customers

"The immediate response I remember from the Celtic fans was, 'How can you put blue on a Celtic shirt?'"

HOME 1984/85

Match worn from the Neilly Mochan collection

While some clubs had been regularly incorporating sponsor logos onto the front of their jerseys since the early 1980s, Celtic – ever protective of the sacred hoops – were relatively late to the party.

Following the resolution of a dispute with the television companies after Hibernian included a Bukta logo on their jerseys in 1977, shirt sponsorship had been allowed only in non-televised matches. But since their matches appeared on the weekly highlights package virtually every weekend, this was not much help to Celtic. In 1983 the broadcasters finally relented and allowed teams to wear sponsor logos in televised matches, albeit at a reduced size of 50 per cent of their regular size (32 inches squared).

A year later, after signing a joint Old Firm deal with Dunfermline-based double-glazing firm CR Smith which would see the company sponsor both Celtic and Rangers, a patch of white material bearing the sponsor's logo in black was stitched onto the third green hoop from the top of the previous season's home shirt.

The first CR Smith jersey made its debut on 29th September 1984 in a 3-2 league win over Dundee at Dens Park and it was worn right up until the final league game of the season. Over the course of the season two different versions of the jersey were worn, with the CR Smith logo allowed to be larger for non-televised matches. However, this seems to have been fairly randomly regulated and there are matches when some players are wearing jerseys with the smaller logo whilst others have the larger version.

The white sponsor's patch looked unsightly to some Celtic supporters and they made their misgivings known on the letters pages of the *Celtic View*. The club, however, was not backed by wealthy businessmen in the 1980s, and with the European glory days of the sixties and seventies a distant memory any new income streams had to be considered.

Above: Davie Provan strides across the turf, with the white patch for the CR Smith logo visibly protruding from the shirt front

Right: This jersey, featuring a black number and a smaller logo to conform with regulations, was prepared for a European match

CR SMITH

AWAY 1984-86

Match worn by Derek Whyte

This lime green away jersey is one of the most-loved Celtic shirts of all time. Not just because of the design, but because of the events that unfolded when it was worn at Love Street, Paisley, on 3rd May 1986.

This was the final day of the 1985/86 league season. Leaders Hearts only required a draw at home against Dundee to secure the title, while Celtic would have to beat St Mirren by three goals and hope that Hearts lost in order to win the league. Sensationally, as the afternoon unfolded, Celtic overran St Mirren 5-0 while Hearts lost 2-0 to Dundee. This incredible league title win is often simply referred to as 'Love Street '86'.

The jersey featured on these pages is from the Neilly Mochan collection, and is believed to have been worn by Derek Whyte on that historic day.

First released in 1983, this away jersey first appeared with the CR Smith logo for the club's European Cup Winners' Cup first round second leg tie against KAA Gent on 3rd October 1984 – just four days after the first sponsored edition of the hoops made its debut.

The standout performer for Celtic in the match against Gent was Frank McGarvey, who scored a brace at Celtic Park as the Belgians were knocked out 3-1 on aggregate.

In the famous match at Love Street 18 months later – the last occasion when this jersey style was worn – McGarvey was plying his trade at St Mirren, and he was later accused by some Hearts players of not giving everything in the league-deciding game. More than 30 years later, McGarvey – who is a lifelong Celtic fan – retorted that he had given maximum effort against his former club but that "the champagne in the Celtic dressing room after the game could have been better".

Above: The celebrations in the Celtic dressing room at Love Street have since entered into club legend

Left: A rare long-sleeved version of this jersey style

AWAY 1984/85

Player shirt from the Neilly Mochan collection

Umbro provided Celtic with an 'emergency' kit for their European Cup Winners' Cup second round first leg tie against Rapid Vienna in Austria on 24th October 1984. This was needed because the Austrian team's green-and-white striped home shirts clashed with both of Celtic's kits.

To create the jersey, Umbro used the same template as they had employed for the Arsenal away strip of 1984/85 (which featured the main body in yellow with dark blue trim), a kit that the Gunners had worn at Celtic Park in a friendly 'challenge' match earlier that season.

The main body of the shirt was yellow, but with subtle vertical 'shadow' stripes. The v-neck collar, cuffs, numbering, CR Smith and Umbro logos were all applied in green to complete what was a simple but striking design. The shorts and socks were also green and the club crest and Umbro emblem both featured on the right side of the shorts.

Because this jersey style was only worn on a handful of occasions, it is an extreme rarity in match worn collector circles (and was sadly never released as a replica strip). However, it did feature in one of the most controversial European ties in the club's history.

Celtic lost 3-1 away to Rapid Vienna in what was an ill-tempered first-leg. Although they turned around this deficit at Celtic Park by winning 3-0, Davie Hay's men were forced by UEFA to replay the match at a neutral venue after a bottle was thrown on to the pitch from the famous Jungle terracing. The second leg was replayed at Old Trafford in a match won by Rapid – who would go on to reach the final – by a single goal.

This scarcely worn kit made other fleeting appearances (with yellow socks) but it is difficult to determine any further information regarding the featured jersey as it has no number on the back and was therefore not match worn.

With Rapid Vienna in green and white stripes, Celtic required this yellow 'emergency' kit for the away leg of this controversial European Cup Winners' Cup tie

SCOTTISH CUP FINAL 1985

Match worn by Mo Johnston

The 100th Scottish Cup Final was a special occasion and the SFA pulled out all the stops to celebrate it as such: pipe bands, a parade and an introduction of winning captains of yesteryear, including Jock Stein, Kenny Dalglish and Billy McNeill.

Celtic marked the event by turning out in a brand-new strip that would be worn the following season, a marketing strategy that would become increasingly common around this time. The seven-hooped design was similar to the previous version of the hoops, but most notably featured a contemporary crossover round-necked collar. In addition, and for this match only, the CR Smith logo was applied in black flock on a white hoop rather than appearing on a white patch on top of a green hoop.

The jersey also features embroidered commemorative match detail in black beneath the club crest, and an embroidered Umbro logo.

Dundee United took the lead in the final on 55 minutes when Stuart Beedie beat Pat Bonner low down at his left-hand post. With 15 minutes remaining, Murdo MacLeod was fouled about 25 yards from Hamish McAlpine's goal. In the commentary box, legendary commentator Archie Macpherson announced, "In the whole history of Scottish Cup Finals, only two goals have ever been scored directly from free-kicks." A few seconds later, Davie Provan's swerving strike hurtled inches under the crossbar and into the net to make it three.

In the previous season's final, Roy Aitken had been sent off during the defeat to Aberdeen. This time he was imperious, hooking over an inch-perfect cross six minutes from time that Frank McGarvey headed into the net for the winner. It was to be the last time that McGarvey ever touched a ball for the club.

The featured jersey is part of the Neilly Mochan collection and was worn by Maurice 'Mo' Johnston, who was the only Celtic player to wear long-sleeves on the day. Just four years later, Mo signed for Rangers, which has resulted in his match worn Celtic jerseys being less sought-after.

Above: Mo Johnston is pictured during Celtic's 2-1 victory over Dundee United in the 100th Scottish Cup Final

Right: The short-sleeved version of this shirt, which was favoured by Johnston's team-mates

HOME 1985-87

Match worn from the Neilly Mochan collection

The home jersey first worn in the 1985 Scottish Cup Final was worn for the following two seasons – although the 1982-85 style returned briefly during the 1985/86 pre-season.

Apart from the lack of match-detail embroidery, the standard-issue jerseys also saw the return of the white patch to house the CR Smith logo. Locating the logo on the white patch meant it could be positioned higher up the jersey – and therefore was more likely to be visible in post-match player interviews and pen pics – than the version on the cup final jersey which was located lower down within a white hoop.

From December 1985, the version with larger sponsor lettering was increasingly used as the television broadcasters became used to the idea of sponsorship and relaxed their rules. By now it was only obligatory to use the smaller sponsor logo in European competitions due to stricter UEFA regulations.

As can be seen on the jersey pictured opposite, with the relatively thin hoops the larger sponsor logo almost completely covers the third green hoop and the black CR Smith lettering overlaps into the white hoops above and below it. The patches were sewn onto the jerseys and the overall effect appeared slightly haphazard in comparison to the jerseys of rival teams.

This style was worn during the European Cup Winners' Cup match against Atlético Madrid, which was played behind closed doors on 2nd October 1985 at the behest of UEFA following the crowd disorder during the infamous match against Rapid Vienna the previous season.

Celtic officially wore this home kit until the end of the 1986/87 season before it was passed down to the reserves, but it made several further cameo appearances following that trophyless campaign.

Above: Roy Aitken in action, wearing the version of this shirt with the larger CR Smith logo

Right: An example of the same jersey with the smaller sponsor's logo, obligatory for European matches

AWAY 1986-87

Match worn by Paul McStay

Yellow was once again chosen as the main colour for Celtic's new change kit, launched at the start of the 1986/87 season.

This canary yellow jersey featured a green and white crossover v-neck collar and green cuffs with white trim, and the front of the shirt incorporated a subtle diamond 'shadow' pattern. Green piping separated the sleeves from the main body of the jersey at the shoulders.

The new design was first worn in a European Cup first round, first leg against Shamrock Rovers on 17th September 1986, even though the white, green and black third jersey launched at the same time had been designated as the European alternative.

The style was worn for three seasons, albeit in two different incarnations. From December 1987 the crest was changed to the 'celtic cross' centenary badge that also appeared on the home jersey between 1987 and 1989 and the version featured on these pages was never worn again.

There were also other slight variations to the jerseys of this design, with some match worn examples having Umbro embroidered in lower case letters under the 'double diamond' logo, whilst others had just the logo with no lettering. The CR Smith logo and number on the back were also applied in green on some versions.

Celtic wore this shirt style in the infamous league match at Easter Road on 28th November 1987 when a gas canister was thrown into the Hibs' fans' area, resulting in a situation that the police described as a "near-disaster" as 45 people were taken to hospital.

The No.8 jersey featured here was regularly worn by Paul McStay, who developed into the country's finest midfielder during the mid-to-late eighties, winning Scotland's Player of the Year accolade in 1987/88.

Above: A muddy Mo Johnston and Peter Grant celebrate victory over Hibs at Easter Road

Right: This long-sleeved example features an Umbro logo without the company's name

CRSMITH

THIRD 1986/87

Match worn by Anton Rogan

Celtic's bold change strip for the 1986/87 season – billed as a 'European' kit – was barely used by the first team and has consequently become a real rarity amongst collectors. Its origins are also unique as the jersey was designed by a 13-year-old supporter.

In 1985, fanatical Celtic-supporting schoolboy Simon Weir – now a successful actor who has appeared in films including *The Acid House* and *Trainspotting 2* – used his felt-tipped pens to draw what he thought would make a great away kit. He was so pleased with his design that he sent it to club manager, Davie Hay, and soon received a reply.

"He thanked me for the design," explained Simon to the *A Celtic State of Mind* podcast more than 30 years later, "and wrote, 'I see you are very artistic'. He also must have sent my design to Umbro because I remember getting a letter from them. They told me that they had been given my design by Davie Hay and that they thought it was great."

Simon though that was the end of the matter. But when he saw the team photograph for the 1986/87 season he noticed that half the squad were wearing a very familiar-looking jersey.

"It looked remarkably like the one I designed," he explained. "I had lost the Umbro letter and I didn't have the original design for the jersey that I drew, but as far as I was concerned it was my idea, my design. At the age of 13 I had a bit of a chip on my shoulder about it. But looking back now I'm pretty glad they did it and I can proudly say I designed a Celtic kit."

Not only was this so-called European kit never worn in a European match, in fact it was not worn in a single competitive Celtic game. Its only appearance was in a friendly on 21st July 1988 against SR Delemont on the final match of a Swiss tour and the jersey featured here is believed to have been worn in that match by left-back Anton Rogan.

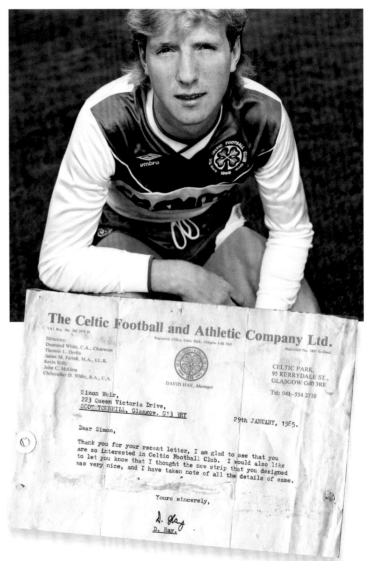

Top: Anton Rogan models the 'European' kit that was never worn in a competitive match

Above: The letter young shirt designer Simon Weir received from Celtic manager Davie Hay

CR SMITH

3

HOME 1987-89 CENTENARY

Match worn by Frank McAvennie

With iconic ex-captain and manager Billy McNeill back at the helm and overseeing a comprehensive rebuilding of the playing squad, Celtic had renewed cause for optimism as they headed into their centenary season. And along with a new-found belief, they had a brand-new set of hoops sporting an eye-catching crest.

The five hoops on the new jersey were thicker than they had ever been before, which meant that the CR Smith logo could be positioned within a single white hoop. The shirt had a shiny harlequin pattern running through the material, a feature shared by many other Umbro jerseys of the period which was now possible due to the advancement of fabric technology. The retro-style collar was a round-neck with single button, the first time a buttoned collar had been used on a home shirt since the 1950s.

The commemorative 'celtic cross' centenary crest that was also introduced was warmly received by supporters, which may have come as some surprise as previous significant changes to the jersey (especially the introduction of the crest in 1977 and a shirt sponsor in 1984) had been widely lambasted. But the centenary design was considered a welcome nod to the green celtic cross within a red circle that had adorned the first Celtic shirts way back in 1888.

Away from the pitch, numerous activities were arranged to celebrate the club's landmark birthday: *The Celtic Story* stage show sold out Glasgow's Pavilion Theatre; Celtic played Brazil's Cruzeiro in a pre-season challenge match; an exhibition to celebrate the Hoops' illustrious history took place at Glasgow's People's Palace; and the centenary crest even appeared as a floral installation at Glasgow's Garden Festival.

With a squad reinforced by the additions of Mick McCarthy (signed by outgoing manager Davie Hay from Manchester City), Chris Morris, Andy Walker, Billy Stark, Joe Miller and Frank McAvennie, the result was a league and Scottish Cup double, with victory repeatedly snatched from the jaws of defeat. One of the finest proponents of that season's 'never say die' attitude was McAvennie, whose match worn jersey is featured here.

Above: Frank McAvennie's determination and knack for last-minute goals proved crucial to Celtic's fortunes in their centenary season

Left: The club's centenary crest proved extremely popular with fans

AWAY 1988 CENTENARY

Match worn from the Paul Lamb collection

While Celtic's centenary crest was introduced to the home shirt for the beginning of the 1987/88 season, it didn't appear on the club's change strip in a match until well into the 1988 calendar year. When it did it was essentially the same yellow away kit that Celtic had used since 1986, but there were some subtle changes along with the introduction of the new badge.

Celtic wore the original version of this shirt – with the four-leaf clover crest and black CR Smith logo – against St Mirren at Love Street in their first away match of 1988. But by the time Billy McNeill's men recorded a 4-0 win against Dunfermline at East End Park on 2nd March 1988, the new crest was in place along with a green CR Smith logo which complemented the collar and sleeve trims as well as the Umbro logo and new green and white crest.

This shirt style was also worn against Hamilton Academical on 5th November 1988, an afternoon where Celtic ran out emphatic 8-0 winners to inflict a record home defeat on their hosts.

It was used again three days later against German champions Werder Bremen in the European Cup. On this occasion, Celtic wore yellow shorts, which gave them an all-yellow look that harked back to their classic kits of 1970/71 and 1977/78. A scoreless draw at the Weserstadion was not enough to claw back the single Thomas Wolter goal scored at Celtic Park a fortnight previously.

The same all-yellow combo featured against St Mirren at Love Street on 26th November 1988, but by the time of the match against Hibernian at Easter Road on 21st January 1989 it had been replaced by a new away kit design.

The small number of occasions on which this jersey was worn has made it almost impossibly rare and much sought-after by collectors of match worn jerseys. It is possible that only one set of strips were ever supplied to Celtic, as they were only used for one calendar year (and fairly sparingly).

Neither this jersey or the yellow alternative shorts were ever available to purchase as part of a replica kit.

Celtic's Chris Morris battles with Andy Watson of Hibs in the centenary version of the yellow away jersey

SCOTTISH CUP FINAL 1988

Match worn from the Neilly Mochan collection

Celtic's centenary hoops received the slightest of additions under the commemorative crest when the match details were embroidered for the Scottish Cup Final against Dundee United on 14th May 1988. This was an encounter that had an air of *deja vu* enshrouding it as it was a rematch of the 1985 final. The game itself proved an eerie replay of the match of three years before with Celtic the cavalier, attacking side and United the superbly well-organised, defensive outfit geared for counter-punching.

United took the lead through speed merchant Kevin Gallacher (grandson of Celtic legend Patsy Gallacher), but as the pendulum swung in Celtic's direction late in the second half the atmosphere inside Hampden Park became electric. The Celtic supporters probably outnumbered their Dundee counterparts by three to one and they were adamant that the 100th anniversary of Celtic's first-ever game (due in a few days' time) would not be ruined by a defeat in a cup final.

The Scottish Cup win of 1988 was the culmination of 100 years of history and indomitable traditions – a century of honour – and it was only fitting that the double was finally clinched a mere 15 minutes after all had seemed lost. More typical than the clarion call of Frank McAvennie's equaliser was the manner in which Celtic's 'never say die' attitude clinched the win in the final minute.

That class of '88 still brings a glint to the eyes of Celtic supporters of a certain vintage. The green and white hoops have rarely appeared so resplendent as they did on that sun-drenched Hampden pitch where, after the 2-1 victory, Tommy Burns uttered those spine-tingling words that have tragically outlived the centenary side's ultimate Celt – "That's what's so special about them. They're there and they're always there. And God bless every one of them."

Paul McStay and Roy Aitken take in the crowd's acclaim as Celtic round off their centenary year in style by lifting the Scottish Cup

S.F.A. CUP FINAL
1987-8

CR SMITH

AWAY 1989-91

Match worn by Paul McStay

Celtic fans were treated to some sublime away shirt designs from Umbro during the 1980s. From the bottle green effort worn in the Bernabeu in 1980 to the white and green pinstriped jerseys made famous by an electrifying young Charlie Nicholas; and from the lime green memories of Love Street to the yellow centenary shirt that Frank McAvennie wore when he scored goals for fun, the club's kit manufacturers had barely put a foot wrong.

However, the away jersey that debuted at Easter Road on 21st January 1989, divided opinion amongst the Celtic supporters in a way that hadn't been experienced since the introduction of a club crest in 1978 and sponsorship in 1984.

Celtic lined up against Hibs wearing yet another yellow jersey. But instead of the simplistic beauty of previous yellow shirts, this one employed an intricate and repetitive two-tone green pattern. The detail resembled computerised arrowheads pointing upwards, just as the club were heading in the opposite direction as Celtic entered a sustained period in the doldrums.

As this new jersey was released for the 1988 Christmas market, it was worn alongside Celtic's home centenary shirt throughout the second half of the disappointing 1988/89 season.

The long-sleeved edition featured on these pages was match worn by Celtic's regular No.8, Paul McStay.

Striker Gerry Creaney in the short-sleeved version of this shirt

SCOTTISH CUP FINAL 1989

Match worn from the Neilly Mochan collection

The final appearance of Celtic's centenary home kit was in the 1989 Scottish Cup Final against Rangers, a match which is most remembered for the nature of the winning goal – and it has to be admitted that Celtic were given the benefit of the doubt on this occasion by referee Bob Valentine.

A few minutes before half-time, Roy Aitken tussled for possession with John Brown of Rangers, which resulted in the ball going out of play. Although the ball had touched Aitken's foot last, Celtic's quick-thinking captain raced to pick it up with such conviction that Valentine was fooled into letting him take the throw-in.

A wrong decision over a midfield throw-in is rarely crucial, but in this case it definitely was. Some of the Gers' rearguard had moved forward out of position, leaving Peter Grant unchallenged as he galloped down the wing. His probing cross was intended for Joe Miller but Richard Gough partially cleared the ball with a header which sent the ball in the direction of his partner in central defence, Terry Butcher, who was jostling with Celtic forward Mark McGhee. Butcher attempted to head the ball to right-back Gary Stevens, who was unaware of Miller lurking nearby. The Rangers right-back attempted to roll the ball back to his goalkeeper and Miller pounced, advancing on Chris Woods and firing a low shot past him.

The 1-0 victory, which denied the Ibrox men a domestic treble, salvaged a disappointing season for Billy McNeill's men. Celtic had failed to strengthen the squad after the centenary double triumph, but in the days leading up to the cup final the club had announced the capture of their former star striker Mo Johnston from Nantes. They had paraded him in the centenary jersey and had even allowed him to travel on the Celtic team bus to Hampden Park to watch the game. In a cruel twist, Johnston decided to renege on his agreement and instead signed for Graeme Souness' Rangers. It was a transfer that sent tremors throughout Scottish football.

Goalscoring hero Joe Miller
celebrates with the Scottish Cup

S.F.A. CUP FINAL
1988/89

CRSMITH

HOME 1989-91

Match worn from the Neilly Mochan collection

The much-loved centenary jersey was last worn in the 1989 Scottish Cup Final on the final day of the 1988/89 season. Celtic's 1-0 victory over Rangers added to the positive feeling amongst fans who were excited at the apparent arrival of prodigal son Maurice Johnston. That all evaporated when Johnston signed for Rangers instead and Celtic supporters were instead forced to lick their wounds with the signing of Polish international Dariusz 'Jacki' Dziekanowski.

The new jersey for the 1989/90 season was another popular effort from the club's long-term kit manufacturer, Umbro. The button remained on the collar, which reverted to a polo shirt-style. There were again five bold green hoops, the large black CR Smith logo within a white hoop and the Umbro logo embroidered in green.

Celtic returned to their four leaf-clover crest, but the only other changes were in the shadow pattern and hoop detail. The fabric of the jersey incorporated a broken-glass effect, and there was also a faint white zigzag throughout the green hoops. These were subtle enough not to be noticed from afar and certainly didn't break the hoops up (which would have undoubtedly caused some consternation among the proudly traditionalist Celtic fans).

Despite the acquisitions of Dziekanowski from Legia Warsaw, Paul Elliott from Pisa and Mike Galloway from Hearts, it soon became clear that Celtic were a club in decline – not only on the pitch but in the boardroom too. It did not help matters when club mainstay Tommy Burns left in December 1989, followed by Roy Aitken a month later. Celtic entered the new decade in disarray. Although they came close to winning domestic cups wearing this kit, they would be beaten Scottish Cup finalists in 1990 (where they were defeated on penalties by Aberdeen) and League Cup finalists in 1991 (defeated 2-1 by Rangers after extra-time).

Tommy Coyne in action in the popular 1989-91 hoops

EUROPE 1989

Match worn by Dariusz Dziekanowski

Celtic's 1989 encounter with Partizan Belgrade – during which the jersey featured here was worn – must rank among the most astonishing matches ever witnessed at Celtic Park. The visitors were relatively unknown to the Scottish press and Celtic fans alike – nobody seemed to know how they played nor who their best players were, but everybody was aware that their countrymen Vojvodina Novi Sad had been Celtic's most difficult opponents during the 1967 European Cup campaign.

Having been overcome 2-1 in Mostar in the first leg of the European Cup Winners' Cup first round tie, Celtic returned to Glasgow on a cold late September night where a little under 50,000 turned up, hoping for the best. They were indeed to see the best – and the worst – of their Celtic team…

Dariusz Dziekanowski had arrived from Legia Warsaw in the pre-season for a fee in the region of £600,000. He had represented Poland in the 1986 World Cup and showed flashes of brilliance in his first dozen games for Celtic, scoring eight goals. The Celtic faithful, still reeling from losing Mo Johnston to Rangers, took their new Polish striker to the heart of the Jungle and christened him 'Jacki'.

As individual European performances go, Jacki's against Partizan takes some beating. He completed his hat-trick on 54 minutes to put Celtic 3-2 up on the night, but the lead lasted just five minutes. Jacki's strike partner, Andy Walker, restored the one-goal cushion after 65 minutes before Dziekanowski put Celtic further ahead with his fourth goal of the evening.

Sadly, Sladan Scepovic (whose son, Stefan, would later play for Celtic) scored the all-important goal in the dying minutes to give Partizan Belgrade the tie on away goals. One journalist summed it up perfectly when he wrote, "A swashbuckling Celtic performance: the forwards swashed, the defence buckled."

Dariusz Dziekanowski is a cult hero among Celtic supporters, thanks to his performance against Partizan Belgrade

HOME 1991/92

Match worn from the Neilly Mochan collection

Celtic fans were sold the idea that their club had moved into a new era following the sacking of club legend Billy McNeill. The Lisbon Lion was replaced by Irishman Liam Brady, who had built a reputation as one of the classiest midfielders in European football during a career that took in spells at Arsenal, Juventus, Sampdoria and Inter Milan.

It was a bold move by the Celtic board – Brady had no managerial experience – and the gatekeepers of the club's bank vault (or 'biscuit tin', as it was mockingly known by supporters) backed their new man. Brady went on a spending spree and brought in million-pound men Tony Cascarino, Gary Gillespie and Tony Mowbray.

The club also introduced new home and away Umbro kits for this new dawn, and these were the first jerseys to be emblazoned with Celtic's second shirt sponsors – Peoples Ford – who claimed to be "the fastest-growing Ford dealer group in the country". The stumbling block with the sponsor was that their logo was red, white and blue.

Peoples did not want to advertise their dealership without the blue and white Ford logo, so Celtic's commercial manager Jack McGinn agreed to the deal. The Peoples Ford match programme advertisements read, "The best deal for everyone", but the Celtic fans largely didn't agree with that sentiment.

Other than the controversial shirt sponsorship, Umbro – who exclaimed in their advertising campaign of the period that, "Win, lose or draw, we always look good" – produced a jersey that was distinguished by a zigzag motif on the right sleeve and shorts. The button-down collar was slightly different to the previous season's design, and the five-green-hooped jersey contained a subtle shadow pattern of diamonds spelling out the word 'Celtic'. The Umbro logo included lower case lettering for the final time on a Celtic jersey.

Despite a promising start to Brady's tenure, early exits from the League and UEFA Cups set the tone for a lacklustre campaign in which Celtic finished in third place, a full 10 points adrift of champions Rangers.

Tommy Boyd wearing the long-sleeved version of this controversial jersey

AWAY 1991/92

Match worn from the Paul Lamb collection

While adidas were serving up classic designs in the early nineties by using their three-stripe motif on the shirt sleeves of a host of clubs and countries, Umbro were pushing the boundaries of shirt design with a series of increasingly complicated and outlandish templates.

Celtic's away jersey of 1991/92 is perhaps the ultimate example of this trend, and divides opinion amongst fans to this day – with many considering it to symbolise a period when the club was being poorly managed by a board of directors who would be removed from office just three years later.

This debate-provoking, zigzagged Umbro template was also bestowed upon several other clubs of the period, in different colours, including Sliema Wanderers of Malta, Oldham Athletic, and Parma of Italy. What made Celtic's version even more controversial was that their commercial manager and chairman, Jack McGinn, had sanctioned the use of a new red, white and blue sponsor. The use of these colours on a Celtic jersey simply beggared belief and illustrated just how out of touch with the fans the board had become.

Looking at this shirt more than 30 years later, it is easy to appreciate why it had fans in an uproar. The lime green section at the bottom is reminiscent of the classic lime green away kit of 1986 and had this been used on the top section then it might have been more palatable. Many regard this as the worst kit in Celtic's history. For others, however, it has become a cult classic.

One match in which this kit was worn tragically illustrates the troubled period it represents. On 23rd November 1991, Tony Cascarino – an expensive flop at Celtic who had failed to impress since arriving in the close season for over £1 million from Aston Villa – careered off the Broomfield pitch in a league match against Airdrie and collided with a police sergeant, who suffered career-ending injuries.

For most Celtic supporters it was a relief that the strip, like Cascarino himself, didn't last beyond one season.

Steve Fulton and John Collins in action against Airdrieonians in 1991, wearing what is widely regarded as Celtic's most controversial kit

HOME 1992/93

Match worn from the Neilly Mochan collection

The last Celtic home jersey without a sponsor arrived for the beginning of the 1992/93 season. The romanticists among Celtic supporters may have welcomed a new set of hoops without advertising plastered across the chest, but in reality this omission simply illustrated the chaos that was ensuing off the pitch, particularly at board level. However, in failing to secure a shirt sponsorship deal, the Celtic board inadvertently allowed Umbro to produce two especially popular additions to the Celtic jersey collection – the 1992/93 away shirt and its home counterpart featured here.

The home shirt was essentially the same jersey as the previous season's, although in addition to lacking a sponsor it now had upper case Umbro lettering under the 'double diamond' logo.

Occasionally (for instance in the League Cup match against Stirling Albion on 12th August 1992), Celtic wore the previous season's lime away socks with this home kit against teams who wore white socks.

This Celtic kit was worn during an unfortunate period in the club's history and the perception of the shirt by supporters may be determined by the players who wore it. Manager Liam Brady's big-money signings such as Tony Cascarino and Gary Gillespie had struggled to make an impact and his bargain basement buys didn't fare much better.

A spirited comeback in the UEFA Cup first round against Cologne, when Celtic overturned a two-goal deficit in Glasgow by winning 3-0, could not make up for the abject failure of yet another trophyless campaign.

But worse was to come the following season…

Gerry Creaney wears the long-sleeved 1992/93 home jersey, most notable for the lack of a sponsor

AWAY 1992-94

Match worn from the Neilly Mochan collection

Just when Celtic fans had almost lost faith in Umbro's away jersey designers, the change kit introduced for the 1992/93 season was unveiled to unanimously positive reviews. This was a template used by Sheffield Wednesday, Nottingham Forest and Northern Ireland, among others. It was completely unrecognisable from Celtic's previous two efforts – an old-fashioned design with a brand-new colour scheme.

The main colour, for the first time in Celtic's history, was black, but this was perfectly off-set by vertical stripes – coloured somewhere between teal and turquoise – which also had a white pinstripe splendidly running through each one. The floppy collar featured a button and the crest was framed by a shield, which was a feature of numerous Umbro designs of that time. A repetitive Celtic crest design was incorporated into the main body of the shirt, and the trimmed black shorts and socks complemented the top perfectly.

This jersey was worn for two seasons, with the first (1992/93) being a period where Celtic had no shirt sponsor. This meant that this was the final sponsorless away jersey that Celtic would ever wear. The following season saw the return of CR Smith and, thankfully, their logo was incorporated in white to complement the classic colour scheme of this design.

Despite being worn during an unsuccessful period in the club's history, this jersey was notably used during UEFA Cup encounters with Cologne (15th September 1992), Young Boys of Berne (with white shorts on 14th September 1993) and Sporting Lisbon (with white shorts and socks on 20th October 1993 and again on 3rd November 1993).

This was a memorable Celtic shirt during a forgettable time for the club, and the introduction of black into the away kit canon was to be a regular fixture over the next 25 years.

Above: Paul McStay battles horrendous conditions away to Airdrie in January 1993

Right: For the 1993/94 season, the familiar name of CR Smith returned to the Celtic jersey

"CELTIC DO NOT PLAY FRIENDLIES"

Celtic's rich tradition of playing testimonials and benefit matches has spawned a number of rare and highly-collectible one off jerseys

Right: Bobby Charlton wore the green and white hoops for Ron Yeats' testimonial match in 1974

Throughout the club's history, Celtic have regularly answered the call of players from other teams who wanted to line up against the green and white hoops for their testimonials, not least because of the huge numbers of well-behaved Celtic fans who would inevitably make their way through the turnstiles. On top of that, such matches tend to be lively, entertaining affairs. As Jock Stein said prior to Billy McNeill's testimonial match against Liverpool in August 1974: "Celtic Football Club do not play friendlies."

The list of players over the decades who have requested Celtic's attendance for their own swansongs is like a 'who's who?' of football royalty: England World Cup winners Bobby Moore and Bobby and Jack Charlton; Arsenal's Tony Adams, Paul Davis and David O'Leary; Liverpool's Ron Yeats, Ronnie Moran and Ian Rush; Manchester United's Ryan Giggs, Mark Hughes, Lou Macari and Bryan Robson; Newcastle United's Peter Beardsley and Alan Shearer; not to mention stars of the European stage such as Vitor Baía and Alfredo Di Stéfano. Ex-Celts Lou Macari, Mick McCarthy and Brian McClair

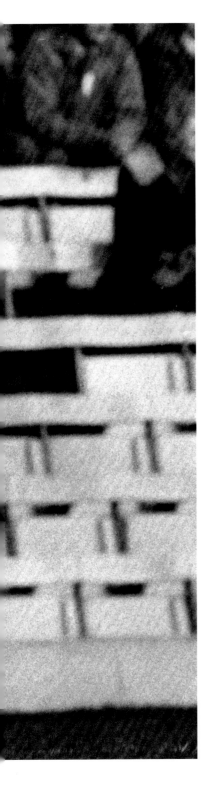

also asked the club to be as special guests for their big nights. Tony Mowbray, Roy Keane and Pat Stanton, meanwhile, enjoyed testimonials for other clubs against the Hoops whilst they were Celtic players.

On some occasions, guest players have turned out in the hoops, much to the delight of the Celtic hordes. Bobby Charlton famously played for Celtic against Liverpool in Ron Yeats' testimonial on 13th May 1974 and opened the scoring in a 4-1 win; Davie Hay returned to Celtic Park on 17th May 1976 to play Manchester United in Bobby Lennox and Jimmy Johnstone's joint testimonial, which resulted in a 4-0 victory; and Kenny Dalglish wore the hoops 10 years after leaving Parkhead as Nottingham Forest defeated Celtic 3-1 in Davie Provan's testimonial on 30th November 1987.

It is also now customary for the jerseys used on these occasions to have bespoke match embroidery, although this was not normal practice prior to Danny McGrain's testimonial on 4th August 1980, so it would be difficult to identify jerseys worn in the tribute games for Jimmy Quinn (1909), Patsy Gallacher (1932), Jimmy McGrory (1934), Willie Maley (1953), Billy McNeill (1974), Jimmy Johnstone and Bobby Lennox (1976) and Jock Stein (1978).

As well as Celtic jerseys from numerous testimonials from 1980 onwards, Neilly Mochan's collection also contains numerous opposition shirts from testimonial games, including Lou Macari's Manchester United top from the 1984 testimonial played at Old Trafford when Macari played the first half for United and the second for Celtic.

Left: Lou Macari's jersey from his testimonial in 1984, when Macari played a half for each team (above)

Right: Celtic played an Ireland XI for Packie Bonner's testimonial at Celtic Park in May 1991

Before the start of his testimonial match against Manchester United, Danny McGrain performed a lap of honour around Parkhead with the Scottish Cup

DANNY McGRAIN TESTIMONIAL

v Manchester United, 4th August 1980

ROY AITKEN TESTIMONIAL

v Manchester United, 25th March 1987

TOMMY BURNS TESTIMONIAL

v Liverpool, 8th August 1987

DAVIE PROVAN TESTIMONIAL

v Nottingham Forest, 30th November 1987

PAUL McSTAY TESTIMONIAL

v Manchester United, 12th December 1995

MIKE GALLOWAY BENEFIT MATCH

v 'All Stars', 3rd March 1996

PETER GRANT TESTIMONIAL

v Bayern Munich, 22nd January 1997

TOM BOYD TESTIMONIAL

v Manchester United, 15th May 2001

THE LISBON LIONS BENEFIT MATCH

v Feyenoord, 22nd January 2003

HENRIK LARSSON TESTIMONIAL

v Sevilla, 25th May 2004

JACKIE McNAMARA TESTIMONIAL

v Republic of Ireland, 29th May 2005

Phil O'Donnell
Tribute Match
Sunday 25th May
2008

PHIL O'DONNELL TRIBUTE MATCH

v Motherwell, 25th May 2008

TOMMY BURNS TRIBUTE MATCH

v Tommy Burns Select XI, 31st May 2009

MAESTRO CHARITY MATCH

*McStay's Maestros v Rio's All Stars,
6th September 2014*

SCOTT BROWN TESTIMONIAL

v Republic of Ireland, 20th May 2018

CHAPTER SIX

THE HOOPS, BUT NOT AS WE KNOW THEM

UMBRO 1993-2005

HOME 1993/94

Match worn from the Neilly Mochan collection

The home jersey that Umbro produced for Celtic's 1993/94 season became era-defining, but not because of any on-field success. This was a period of tumultuous change for the club and Celtic entered the campaign having waved farewell to the famous Jungle terracing on the final day of the previous season. If that loss wasn't enough for Celtic supporters to cope with, they were about to lose a few of their famous hoops as well…

Controversially, Umbro made the bold move of designing a Celtic home shirt which incorporated just four green hoops, of which only three were visible when the round-necked shirt was tucked into the shorts. Not only that, but within each hoop there was a prominent, darker green pattern of haphazard Umbro diamonds, as well as horizontal pinstripes above and below each one (a detail last seen in 1987). The casual observer might point to the fact that it was a classy shirt design, but Celtic supporters are traditionalists and this was never destined to be a fans' favourite.

The introduction of a crest in 1978, of a sponsor in 1984, and now the reduction of hoops infuriated sections of the Celtic fanbase. 'Is there nothing left that is sacred?' some argued. There was more change to follow, too, since this was the last season when the home jersey remained untainted by numbers in domestic matches.

On the pitch, Liam Brady started off his third season as manager with a paltry two league wins from 10 games and promptly resigned, with reserve-team coach and former goalkeeper Frank Connor taking charge until the arrival of 'Quality Street Kid' Lou Macari.

Macari's tenure in the hotseat got off to a winning start with an unlikely 2-1 win at Ibrox on 30th October 1993, although it was said that Connor had prepared the team for this fixture in what was unofficially his final match in charge. Of the thousands of ecstatic Celtic fans in the Broomloan Stand that day, one man from Croy had a vision to revolutionise the club he loved. Five months later, that man – Fergus McCann – saved Celtic from financial collapse.

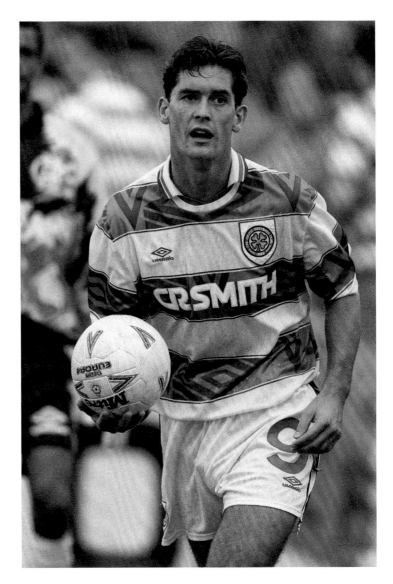

Willie Falconer is pictured in the 1993/94 home shirt with just three hoops visible

HOME 1994/95

Match worn by Brian O'Neil

Following their 1993/94 domestic campaign, Celtic played three friendly matches against Manchester United (Mark Hughes' testimonial), Hearts and Aberdeen. The games against Scottish opposition took place in Ontario, Canada, where Celtic wore a rare variation of their home shirt. This shirt, first seen in the home UEFA Cup tie against Young Boys of Berne earlier that season, had solid green hoops without the darker Umbro pattern. The next change to this Celtic jersey, however, was to be far more significant.

Celtic's aversion to numbers on the green and white hoops can be traced back to Robert Kelly, the club's chairman between 1947 and 1971. Back in 1950, when every other club in Scotland had implemented the numbering system, the autocratic Kelly decided against following suit as he felt that numbers would deface the Celtic jersey. On 14th May 1960 the club first wore numbered shirts for a friendly match against Sparta Rotterdam and by 1975 UEFA had made shirt numbering compulsory for European competitions. However, it wasn't until the start of the 1994/95 season when the Scottish Football Association finally ordered Celtic to add numbers to their shirts for domestic competitions.

Initially, the club complied by adding small black numbers to their sleeves, as seen on the jersey pictured opposite which was worn by Brian O'Neil. This kit was first worn in a league match at Brockville against Falkirk on 13th August 1994. The sleeve numbers were reminiscent of classic North American Soccer League jerseys of the 1960s and 1970s.

The SFA, however, were unimpressed and by the time Celtic faced Rangers at Ibrox in their third league match of the season, green Umbro-branded numbers had been added to the backs of their jerseys.

The hoops would never be quite the same again...

Above: Paul McStay always wore his heart on his sleeve, and for a few games the number 8 also appeared

Right: The back of a later version of the 1994/95 jersey shows the large, green No.8 now applied

AWAY 1994-96

Match worn from the Joe Arcari collection

Celtic mainly wore their black with green and white stripes away kit when required throughout 1994, but this was replaced by yet another predominantly black strip for the league match against Kilmarnock at Rugby Park on 19th November 1994.

The *Celtic View* had asked fans to design a new away strip at the beginning of the year, and most of the submissions that were printed in the 9th March 1994 edition were based on a black, green and white colour scheme. It was clear that this was the *en vogue* colourway among Celtic supporters of the time.

This Umbro template was also used for Chelsea's away kit (in orange and grey), Nottingham Forest's home outfit, and for Manchester United's controversial two-tone grey strip, which was famously blamed by Alex Ferguson for his side's capitulation against Southampton on 13th April 1996. Ferguson believed that his side played poorly because they were unable to pick out their team-mates in the grey kit, and promptly ordered them to change into a blue and white alternative at half-time.

For Celtic's version, Umbro again framed the club crest in a shield, while the top half of the jersey was adorned with white stripes incorporating a black, criss-cross pattern. This detail was repeated on the bottom of the shorts.

This kit was worn on a regular basis domestically and featured in the semi-final of the Scottish Cup against Hibs at Ibrox when Celtic progressed after a replay before going on to win their first trophy in six years. It was also used in testimonials for Ian Rush of Liverpool on 6th December 1994, and by a team of 'Celtic All Stars' in Mike Galloway's testimonial match on 3rd March 1996. In the latter encounter, this jersey adorned such club legends as Kenny Dalglish, Tommy Burns and Roy Aitken.

Paul McStay is challenged by Michael O'Neill as Celtic take on Hibs in the semi-final of the Scottish Cup

THIRD 1994/95

Match worn by Brian McLaughlin

The early nineties was a time of immense change for Celtic, with the club eventually taken over by Fergus McCann in March 1994. After that the club quite literally entered a rebuilding period, with the old Parkhead stadium rising like a phoenix from the flames although that meant that Celtic had to play their home matches at Hampden Park for the entire 1994/95 season.

For this campaign a third kit was introduced, which was unusually worn against teams when there was no real necessity to do so (for instance v Aberdeen on 5th March 1995). It is likely that this jersey was released primarily for commercial reasons, as the black away strip in use at the time could have been worn in all domestic fixtures where there was a clash of colours.

With this somewhat loud white, green and yellow design, Umbro undid a lot of the goodwill gained amongst traditionalist fans that had been gained with the release of the popular black-and-green-striped away kit. Along with mismatched sleeves in yellow and green, Umbro applied large and sporadic zigzagged swooshes to the main body of the shirt, resulting in a distinctive design that didn't sit well with many supporters at the time. Green shorts (featuring yellow and white swooshes) and socks finished the ensemble off.

Worn with distinction by Dutch striker Pierre van Hooijdonk and midfield mainstays John Collins and Paul McStay, this jersey will always be associated with the 'Hampden Season'. This was a transitional period in the club's history, with Celtic finishing fourth in the league and losing to Raith Rovers on penalties in the Scottish League Cup Final but winning the Scottish Cup with a 1-0 victory over Airdrie, with van Hooijdonk – in his first season with the club – scoring the winner.

A hugely sought-after jersey among match worn collectors since it was so rarely worn, the featured shirt is believed to have been worn domestically by winger Brian McLaughlin.

Above: Brian McLaughlin wears the controversial change shirt, which was sometimes worn even when there was no clash with the home jersey

Left: Scottish Football League sleeve patches were first worn during this season

SCOTTISH CUP FINAL 1995

Match worn by Peter Grant

Scottish football's showpiece event of 1995 might not have been a classic, but for Celtic it was of immense importance. It had been six years since the last major trophy had been won, and the final came a little more than six months after a gut-wrenching defeat to Raith Rovers in the League Cup Final. It was no wonder that in the pre-match build-up to the Scottish Cup Final against Airdrieonians – a re-run of the 1975 final – Tommy Burns had mentioned that the pressure was all on Celtic.

When the match arrived, Burns' men took to the Hampden pitch in a new kit, which had been launched just in time for the Celtic support to buy it in their droves ahead of the final. Having been heavily criticised for the presence of just four green hoops on their previous home jersey, Umbro returned to seven hoops for the first time since the 1986/87 season. The traditionalists still weren't entirely satisfied, however, given the fact that the hoops were presented in three different sizes.

The largest central band contained the familiar CR Smith logo, while the hoops included darker green patterns that included the word 'Umbro' and 'Celtic' in celtic script. The crest was again framed by a shield, and the collar was adorned with green and white hoops. With hoops down both sides of the white shorts, and green-and-white-hooped socks for the first time since the 1930s, the overall effect could definitely be described as 'hoop heavy'.

The match was effectively decided as early as the ninth minute when Pierre van Hooijdonk rose to plant a header beyond John Martin in Airdrie's goal. However, the more discerning of observers would save their plaudits for long-serving midfielder Peter Grant, who had so often toiled in the shadows of his more illustrious team-mates Paul McStay and John Collins. Grant had simply refused to give up hope of appearing in the final after suffering knee ligament damage two weeks prior to kick-off, and remarkably recovered in time to make the starting 11 and turn in a sterling performance.

Above: An emotional Peter Grant with manager Tommy Burns after helping secure Celtic's first trophy for six years

Right: A long-sleeved version of the new jersey was also produced for the final, complete with match embroidery

HOME 1995-97

Match worn by Andreas Thom

Having been unveiled in time for the 1995 Scottish Cup Final, this home jersey continued to be worn for a further two seasons of transition at Celtic Park.

Following that triumphant Hampden victory over Airdrieonians, Celtic returned to 'Paradise' on 6th August 1995 for a friendly against Newcastle United. The stadium wasn't fully complete in time for the 1-1 draw with Kevin Keegan's outfit, but a sun-drenched Parkhead was still a more appealing sight than the temporary lodgings of the national stadium.

The £17 million North Stand was also not the only new addition at Celtic Park that day, as German striker Andreas Thom – a £2.2 million capture from Bayer Leverkusen – made his debut. Balancing rebuilding the stadium and the team in tandem was a difficult task for chief executive Fergus McCann, who was under pressure from a record number of Celtic season-ticket holders to further strengthen Tommy Burns' playing squad.

Additional reinforcements did eventually arrive the following year in the form of Portuguese international striker Jorge Cadete and maverick Italian Paolo Di Canio. But sadly, despite the box-office signings, no further silverware was won while wearing this outfit.

Celtic continued to wear this kit when they travelled to the Netherlands for their 1997/98 pre-season tour. However, with the sponsorship deal with CR Smith having ended at the conclusion of the 1996/97 season, the club took the unusual step of adding 'Celtic FC' to their shirts in place of the sponsor's logo.

Andreas Thom gets on the ball in the 'hoop heavy' 1995-97 strip

AWAY 1996-98

Match worn by Pierre van Hooijdonk

For the 1997/98 season, Umbro produced one of the most popular Celtic away jerseys of all time with a design that came to be affectionately referred to by fans as 'The Bumblebee'. It swiftly became a cult classic.

The original Bumblebee (with CR Smith sponsor's logo) made its debut at Lansdowne Road for Mick McCarthy's testimonial against the Republic of Ireland on 26th May 1996, but it made a far more memorable appearance three months later in a league match at Rugby Park against Kilmarnock. New Italian signing Paolo Di Canio was introduced on 57 minutes with Celtic trailing 1-0. Four minutes later, the former AC Milan and Juventus forward equalised for Tommy Burns' side. Di Canio, alongside Pierre van Hooijdonk, Jorge Cadete and Andreas Thom, then went on to inspire Celtic to a 3-1 victory in the rain.

The jersey saw the crest return to the centre of the chest for the first time in nearly 20 years. It was again stationed within an oversized shield with a lime green background. This lime was also used on the black and yellow button-down collar. The yellow and black hoops were of differing thicknesses, and instead of the familiar 'double diamond' logo the manufacturer trademark merely consisted of the word 'Umbro' embroidered above the crest. Somewhat randomly, 'Celtic FC' was also embroidered in black on one of the yellow hoops to the bottom of the shirt. The yellow and black hoops also featured on the socks and down the sides of the black shorts.

Celtic also wore the Bumblebee when Henrik Larsson made his debut against Hibernian on 3rd August 1997, by which time the logo of the club's new sponsor, Umbro, had replaced the CR Smith branding.

Above: Pierre van Hooijdonk gets airborne against Clyde as Jorge Cadete (No.11) looks on

Right: A version of the jersey with 'Umbro' sponsorship was worn during the 1997/98 season

PRE-SEASON 1997/98

The pre-season of 1997/98 provided Celtic with an incoming manager in the shape of Wim Jansen, who joined up with his new squad of players at their Dutch training camp on the outskirts of Arnhem just days after his appointment. Jansen arrived back in his homeland in time to see his Celtic team annihilate amateur side FC Beatrix 21-0 in preparation for their UEFA Cup qualifier later that month.

It was a time of upheaval for Celtic, who were without star players Jorge Cadete and Paolo Di Canio, who had both refused to travel to the Netherlands (Cadete was unwell and Di Canio was in dispute with the club). As well as the changing faces in the dugout, the jerseys were also in transition.

With the club's sponsorship deal with CR Smith having concluded at the end of the 1996/97 campaign, Celtic took the unusual decision to produce two temporary shirts for their three friendly matches on Dutch soil. Rather than appearing sponsorless, the home and away shirts instead featured 'Celtic FC' in place of CR Smith.

The home jersey was worn in Jansen's debut match in charge, as well as in the 8-0 drubbing of VV Veere three days later. It also made an appearance in the first-half of the 3-0 victory over Groningen, but there was a clash of green and white, which resulted in Celtic changing into their unique version of the 'Bumblebee' kit (*right*) at the interval.

Match worn by
Jackie McNamara
v Groningen

The 'Celtic FC' version of the
'Bumblebee' jersey was worn
during the second half of the
tour match against Groningen

HOME 1997-99

Match worn by Harald Brattbakk

Celtic had not won the league title since their centenary year and, to make matters worse, Rangers had wrapped up nine consecutive titles since then to equal Jock Stein's 1966-74 record. The Parkhead club needed something to rekindle the glories of their past. Perhaps a shirt reminiscent of the 1978/79 classic would do the trick?

Early images of the new home shirt appeared in *Shoot!* magazine featuring the CR Smith logo, and at least one rare example of this prototype version is known to have found its way into Celtic shirt collector circles. However, by the time that the new season commenced Celtic had secured a deal with Umbro, who undertook the dual role of kit manufacturer and main sponsor for two seasons.

A welcome return to a more classical design, this jersey returned to the more traditional seven green hoops, although four of these did incorporate a huge two-tone Celtic crest. The collar was a 1970s throwback with 'Celtic' woven across the front of the v-insert, and the four-leaf clover crest appeared in the centre of a home strip for the first time since 1979. The shorts were plain white, with the socks featuring green tops and two green hoops.

While wearing this shirt – which was sized on the large side, reflecting the 'Britpop' fashion for baggy clothing – Celtic embarked on a mission to prevent their free-spending Ibrox rivals from winning their 10th title in a row, and they did so with a new manager, Dutchman Wim Jansen, in charge. Jansen recruited well, in particular attracting the services of Swedish striker Henrik Larsson, who went on to inspire his new side to a famous league and League Cup double in a season that was dramatically drawn out until the last day.

Larsson, of course, is now regarded as a true Celtic legend, whilst Harald Brattbakk, whose jersey features here, attained cult status after scoring in the 2-0 victory over St Johnstone that secured Celtic the league title.

Harald Brattbakk in full flight at Celtic Park against Kilmarnock in September 1998

AWAY 1998-2000

Match worn by Alan Stubbs

Celtic unveiled a new black away jersey before the start of the 1998/2000 season. The reintroduction of lime green to the away kit proved a masterstroke, and in the opinion of many Celtic fans this shirt has aged particularly well.

The original version of this jersey originally included subtle sublimated Celtic crests within the black material, along each of the lime green hoops. However, these were not included on the players' shirts for the UEFA Cup (as can be seen on the featured jersey, which was worn by Alan Stubbs against FC Zurich in Switzerland on 3rd November 1998), which may have been due to strict UEFA rules on the number of club crests allowed.

The 1998/99 season saw the introduction of squad names and numbers to the domestic jerseys, however these were not required for European competition.

The crest on this jersey was centrally placed as it was on the home design. However, it was embroidered in one colour (lime green) on a black background – rather than having the traditional green, white and black badge embroidered in full (as had been a consistent feature of the shirt since 1977) – which made it integral to the jersey's smart and pleasing aesthetic,

Jozef Vengloš – who had succeeded Wim Jansen as Celtic manager in July 1998 – left the club after just one season in charge and former England international John Barnes took the helm for the 1999/2000 campaign. Celtic kept their popular black and lime green away kit for this campaign but by now they had a new shirt sponsor in NTL.

The NTL version of this jersey was worn on the fateful night of 21st October 1999 against Olympique Lyonnais in the UEFA Cup when Henrik Larsson suffered a horrific leg break after 19 minutes. The loss of Larsson was undoubtedly the turning point of Barnes' Celtic tenure. By the time that the Swedish international returned to the first team on the final day of the season, Barnes had long been sacked after a string of disappointing results.

Above: Alan Stubbs celebrates scoring against Portugal's Vitoria Guimaraes in the UEFA Cup while wearing the European version of this jersey without the multiple sublimated crests (right)

Right: An example of the NTL-sponsored variant with multiple Celtic crests subtly visible along each horizontal stripe

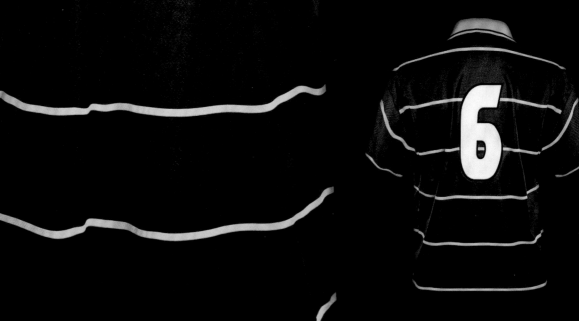

HOME 1999-2001

Match worn by Mark Burchill

The arrival of John Barnes as head coach in June 1999 was a bold move by Celtic. The inexperienced Barnes would be assisted by Kenny Dalglish as director of football operations as part of a 'dream team' managerial line-up that quickly turned into a nightmare.

In an effort to prise the league trophy out of Rangers' grip, the new management team bought big as the arrivals of Stiliyan Petrov, Eyal Berkovic, Olivier Tebily and Rafael Scheidt put a near-£15 million dent in the Celtic Park coffers.

These new signings lined up in a new Celtic home jersey that was reminiscent of their vintage eighties designs. After a period of nineties over-indulgence, Umbro went back to basics, with the result being an uncomplicated kit that has stood the test of time.

The seven untarnished hoops were solid green – no patterns or shading, no quirks. The neck was essentially a round-neck, but it was layered to resemble a shallow v-neck. The crest returned to the left breast and the Umbro 'double diamond' returned to the right.

In addition, a new sponsor – cable television firm NTL – made their first appearance on the hoops, although their logo was housed in a white rectangle that broke the central hoop (a bone of contention from back in the earliest CR Smith days).

After 12 wins in his first 13 competitive matches, John Barnes would have gone into the UEFA Cup second round tie away to Lyon on 21st October 1999 full of confidence, particularly on the back of a resounding 7-0 defeat of Aberdeen five days earlier. Unfortunately, Henrik Larsson suffered a horror leg-break in France as Celtic lost to a solitary goal and Barnes' management career – like Celtic's season – went into freefall.

With the advent of the Scottish Premier League, the previous campaign – 1998/99 – had seen the introduction of squad names and numbers, and from the following season the jerseys also carried 'Bank of Scotland SPL' sleeve patches.

Striker Mark Burchill in action against Inverness in the classically clean 1999-2001 hoops

OLD FIRM MATCH 1999

Match prepared for Morten Wieghorst

Although forever tarnished by the memory of Celtic's 3-1 capitulation against Inverness Caledonian Thistle in the Scottish Cup on 8th February 2000 – immortalised by *The Sun*'s famous 'Super Caley Go Ballistic Celtic Are Atrocious' headline – this jersey was also memorably worn in what was billed as 'The Final Old Firm Match of the Millennium' on 27th December 1999.

Legendary commentator Archie Macpherson described the atmosphere of this fixture just before kick-off as being "a cacophony of undiluted hatred". The match itself, however, was of the highest quality. Mark Viduka put Celtic ahead in 18 minutes with a spectacular strike following a neat pass from Eyal Berkovic, but Rangers' Billy Dodds equalised within 10 minutes with a deflected snapshot past Jonathan Gould.

A draw was perhaps the correct result but after over a 100 years of conflict on the pitch there was no inkling among these Glasgow giants, as they moved into a new century, that the fixture wouldn't last another century. Thirteen years later, Rangers would suffer a financial collapse that sent them into liquidation. Since then, the majority of Celtic supporters no longer refer to the fixture against Rangers as being the 'Old Firm Derby' (although, for commercial reasons, broadcasters and the press still use the term).

The featured shirt was match prepared for Morten Wieghorst, although the Danish international didn't feature in the game.

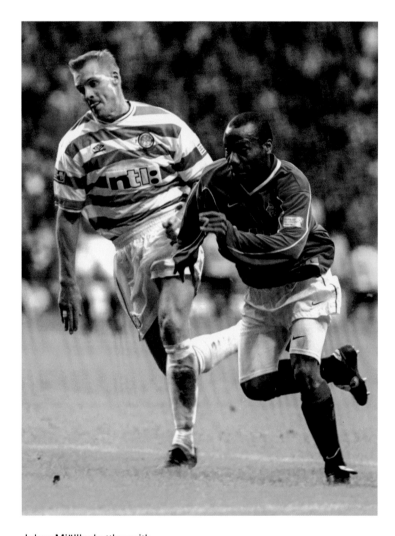

Johan Mjällby battles with
Rod Wallace during the final
Rangers v Celtic match of the
Millennium in December 1999

AWAY 2000/01

Match worn by Johan Mjällby

The 2000/01 season saw the arrival of Martin O'Neill to Celtic Park, and the Northern Irishman's side took the field for a pre-season friendly against FC Copenhagen in Denmark on 12th July 2000 wearing a new yellow away jersey.

Umbro had successfully used this colour scheme for Celtic change kits as far back as 1970 and the decision to return to yellow tops, green shorts and socks was a popular move with the fans. The dark green used for the v-neck and cuffs was also used for the single-colour crest embroidery and Umbro logo, as well as the NTL sponsor's logo. The only additional details on this shirt were two green stripes down each side on both the front and back of the jersey.

O'Neill's competitive tenure got off to a winning start at Tannadice on 30th July 2000 when, unusually, both clubs lined-up in their away kits – Dundee United in green and Celtic in yellow. Goals from a fully recovered Henrik Larsson and debutant Chris Sutton (who had completed a club record £6 million transfer from Chelsea) sealed a 2-1 victory for a Celtic side that went on to win a domestic treble for the first time since 1969.

Just as they had done in 1977, Celtic faced Luxembourg side Jeunesse d'Esch in Europe wearing yellow away jerseys. A comprehensive 11-0 victory over two legs of the UEFA Cup first round marginally bettered their 11-1 victory of 23 years earlier.

This change kit was also worn in both domestic cup finals in Martin O'Neill's first season in charge. Celtic won the League Cup after Henrik Larsson scored a hat-trick in a 3-0 final victory over Kilmarnock on 18th March 2001.

Hibs were defeated by the same scoreline two months later in the Scottish Cup Final, where that man Larsson added another two goals to Jackie McNamara's 39th-minute opener. After the final whistle, the players changed into a set of home jerseys so that they were photographed lifting the trophy in the famous hoops.

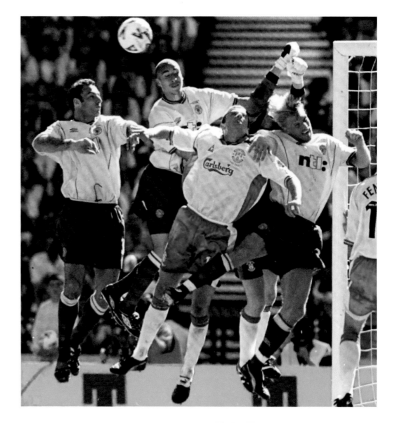

Above: Ramon Vega, Henrik Larsson and Johan Mjällby battle for the ball in the Hibs penalty area during the 2001 Scottish Cup Final

Right: Mjällby lifts the cup, the whole team having changed into a set of hoops for the trophy lift

HOME 2001-03

Match worn by Alan Thompson

Martin O'Neill replaced interim manager Kenny Dalglish for the beginning of the 2000/01 campaign and quickly shelled out nearly £10 million to secure the services of Belgian international Joos Valgaeren and Chelsea striker Chris Sutton.

The impact was immediate, but the launch of the club's new home kit was less so. This 2000/01 strip was not worn competitively until 4th April 2001 in a 2-1 league win against Dundee. The club had access to the new kits long before then, as they were worn against Tampa Bay Mutiny in a friendly match on 20th January 2001, so the reason for the decision not to wear the new jerseys until the final nine domestic games of the season is not known.

By the time this jersey was finally unveiled at Celtic Park, O'Neill had already won the League Cup by virtue of a 3-0 victory over Kilmarnock, which saw Henrik Larsson net a hat-trick. The league was wrapped-up a week after this shirt made its competitive debut following a 1-0 win against St Mirren, and the treble was completed when Hibs were disposed of 3-0 in the Scottish Cup Final.

Celtic had won both cups wearing their yellow change kit, but they completed a quick costume change into their home shirts before Paul Lambert and Tom Boyd led their side up the Hampden Park steps to be presented with the Scottish Cup.

A white underarm panel, which stretched down each side of the shirt, broke up the hoops on this jersey – much to the dissatisfaction of purist supporters who otherwise acknowledged this was a stylish and popular design.

Alan Thompson reveals the white underarm panel which was criticised by some supporters

AWAY 2001/02

Match worn by Chris Sutton

Although the 2000/01 yellow change kit continued to make appearances during the following season (most notably against Ajax for the Champions League qualifier in Amsterdam on 8th August 2001), a new change strip was launched in the summer of 2001 for Martin O'Neill's treble winners.

The new jersey was almost completely white, with a single green stripe that ran from the neck and down the front of each arm. The collar had a black trim and underside, while the Umbro logo was now a stretched version of the manufacturer's 'double diamond' emblem without any text. The club crest returned to a full three-colour embroidered design on the left breast. The shorts and socks were predominantly black which worked well with the white top.

This jersey was first worn in a league match against Hibernian at Easter Road on 25th August 2001 when both clubs wore change kits (Hibs were in purple). This fixture was once referred to as the 'Battle of the Greens' with both clubs traditionally wearing their home kits for these encounters, but those days are now long gone.

On this occasion, Celtic raced into a four-goal lead in just over half-an-hour with goals from Lubomír Moravcík, Chris Sutton (who bagged two) and Henrik Larsson. It was a vintage performance in what is now regarded as a vintage change strip.

Like some other modern Celtic shirts, this is an incredibly sought-after match worn jersey due to its limited number of appearances. Replica versions included embroidery under the club crest to commemorate the previous season's treble-winning success.

The shirt featured on these pages was worn by Chris Sutton. It was originally framed and the mounting glue has unfortunately left marks on what is a real match worn rarity.

Chris Sutton slams home
Celtic's second goal against
Hibs in August 2001

AWAY 2002-2004

Match prepared for Neil Lennon

The 2001/02 white away jersey was sandwiched between two very similar change kits. Both were yellow with green detail and shorts but the new kit – launched before the 2002/03 season – featured a crossover neck, green panels under the arms and was worn with yellow socks rather than green.

The new change shirt also carried a different sponsor's logo than previous NTL kits, the branding incorporating the text 'NTL: Home Digital TV'. The club crest was once again embroidered in one colour – dark green – which was a feature of Umbro's later Celtic away jersey designs.

This shirt style was first worn in a pre-season friendly on 7th July 2002 against the green and white hoops of Shamrock Rovers, but it will always be synonymous with Celtic's famous run to the 2003 UEFA Cup Final.

Martin O'Neill's march to Celtic's third European final began with a disappointing exit from the Champions League at the hands of Basel, who eliminated the Glasgow side on away goals after a 3-3 draw over two legs.

The yellow away jersey then featured on the road in the UEFA Cup against FK Suduva, Blackburn Rovers, Celta Vigo, VfB Stuttgart, and Boavista. The hoops were worn in the quarter-final against Liverpool, and in the final defeat to José Mourinho's Porto in Seville.

Sets of away jerseys were prepared for the final, complete with match-detail embroidery, in case Celtic's favoured hoops were deemed to clash with Porto's blue and white stripes. In the event, however, the hoops were allowed and the yellow tops were not needed. The shirt pictured here is Neil Lennon's Seville-prepared but unworn long-sleeved shirt

Although a new black and gold away kit was launched by Umbro for the following season, this yellow strip was retained as a third kit, with the new Carling sponsor in position. This minor change added a flash of black, green and white to the jersey.

Above: Neil Lennon drives forward as Celtic take on VfB Stuttgart in the 2003 UEFA Cup

Right: The 2003/04 version of this shirt, complete with Carling sponsor's logo on the chest

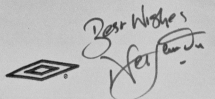

UEFA CUP FINAL 2003

Match worn by Didier Agathe

It was very much appropriate that, having reached their first major European final in more than 30 years, Celtic took to the field – in front of a veritable wall of passionate fans who had made the journey to Seville – in a brand-new jersey reminiscent of the iconic hoops worn on the historic night in 1967 when the club became the first British winners of a European trophy.

Having begun the competition using the 2001-03 home jersey – which featured six green hoops – it was fitting that the new style reverted to the classic seven hoops, as well as featuring a round-neck collar not at all dissimilar to the Lisbon Lions shirts. The button-up collar also evoked memories of the 1987-89 centenary shirt, while the celtic cross used on that design made a reappearance on the back of the jersey to mark the club's 115th year. In short, it was most certainly a jersey that was worthy of the occasion.

Unfortunately, the story did not come full circle with Martin O'Neill's side losing the final to José Mourinho's Porto in extra-time. However, the heartbreaking defeat in the Estadio de La Cartuja on 21st May 2003 is still considered by many Celtic supporters as one of the football highlights of their lives. The city of Seville had never seen anything like it as more than 75,000 Celtic fans descended upon the city from all over the world.

The jersey featured here was worn in the final by Didier Agathe, whose pinpoint cross early in the second half was brilliantly headed home by Henrik Larsson to make it 1-1. Larsson scored a second header to equalise again and take the pulsating match into extra-time, but Bobo Baldé's sending off left Celtic firmly up against it in the additional period.

Martin O'Neill's men hung on grimly until five minutes from the end when a pass from Deco opened up their rearguard. Although Rab Douglas parried the eventual shot, Derlei followed up and clipped the ball beyond the helpless Celtic keeper. It was a sad ending to a magnificent campaign that so nearly brought another European trophy back to Celtic Park.

Above: Didier Agathe's rampaging runs from wing-back made him popular with Celtic fans, but even his efforts weren't quite enough in the 2003 UEFA Cup Final

Right: The UEFA Cup sleeve patch, which was worn on the right arm

HOME 2003/04

Match worn by John Hartson

Following the disappointment of the UEFA Cup Final defeat at the hands of Porto, Celtic retained the kit that had been introduced for that European finale for the 2003/04 season, although the shirt sponsorship transferred from NTL to beer brand Carling.

Seven green hoops adorned a jersey that celebrated 100 years since Celtic introduced what had become an iconic design, and the hoops featured a subtle shadow-effect to give them a modern twist. To commemorate '100 Years of the Hoops', as well as 115 years of the club, the celtic cross crest from the centenary kit was positioned on the rear of this shirt, just below the neckline.

To the eternal sadness of everyone connected to Celtic Football Club, legendary Swedish striker Henrik Larsson decided to leave Parkhead at the end of the 2003/04 double-winning campaign. 'The Magnificent Seven' signed off with a brace in the 3-1 Scottish Cup Final victory against Dunfermline and bade farewell at his testimonial three days later against Sevilla. The jersey pictured opposite was worn in that game by powerful Welsh striker John Hartson.

In the pre-season of 2004/05, Celtic faced Roma on the final date of their North American tour, and a third variation of this jersey was used on what was to be the last occasion that the kit was worn. Instead of Carling, club sponsors Molson Coors requested that 'Coors Light' – a more recognisable beer brand to the local audience – be advertised on the shirt. Somewhat surprisingly, the red, white and black logo was aesthetically pleasing when placed against the green and white background.

Above: John Hartson tussles with a Sevilla defender in Henrik Larsson's testimonial match

Right: The one-off 'Coors Light' version of this jersey, worn v Roma during the club's North American tour in 2004

HENRIK LARSSON GAME
v
SEVILLE
25-05-2004
THE CELTIC FOOTBALL CLUB
1888
CARLING

HARTSON
10

AWAY 2003/04

Match worn by Henrik Larsson

Umbro's marketing slogan for their 2003/04 Celtic away kit was 'Black Magic'. The advertising campaign stated that they had "conjured up a fantastic new design" and showed Neil Lennon posing in the centre of a huge gold club crest, with team-mates Stiliyan Petrov and Shaun Maloney flanking him on both sides. The expressions on the faces of the three players were serious, if slightly contrived, while the kit was quite simply stunning.

The beauty of this kit was in its simplicity. The whole strip was mainly black with gold detail. The collar was reminiscent of the club's seventies jerseys, and the Carling sponsor's logo continued the theme with gold flashes replacing the traditionally red segments usually contained within the design. This kit is regarded as one of Umbro's finest Celtic away strips of the modern era.

The 'Black Magic' kit made its debut appearance in the first leg of a Champions League qualifier against Lithuanian side Kaunas on 30th July 2003. Henrik Larsson (whose domestic match worn jersey is pictured opposite) scored the first of Celtic's four goals in 12 minutes to take his European tally for the Hoops to 30, which equalled the British goalscoring record for any player for a single club in European competition.

It was fitting that the Swedish icon made history on the night that Celtic paid tribute to their greatest team – The Lisbon Lions – by adding a gold star above their four-leaf clover crest. This was the first Celtic jersey to feature a star to commemorate the club's historic European Cup success of 1967, a classy design feature which had been suggested to the club by a creative fan.

Henrik Larsson and Bobo Baldé take the acclaim of the Celtic supporters after a victory over Kilmarnock in April 2004

AWAY 2004/05

Match worn by Johan Mjällby

The final Umbro away jersey worn by Celtic was delivered in time for the 2004 Scottish Cup Final, as the Hoops faithful prepared to bid farewell to 'The King of Kings', Henrik Larsson.

Umbro had prophetically announced in their marketing campaign for the new kit that 'Green = Silverware', and they were not wrong when it came to the club's encounter with Dunfermline Athletic at Hampden Park on 22nd May 2004.

Despite the Fifers taking the lead through Andrius Skerla five minutes before the break, Larsson took control of proceedings in the second half when he grabbed a brace to put Celtic ahead. Stiliyan Petrov rounded off the scoring to secure a league and Scottish Cup double in Larsson's final competitive appearance in a Celtic jersey.

The jersey itself was not such an overwhelming success as its 'Black Magic' predecessor. The concept seemed sound enough – dark green with silver detail – but it didn't seem to find great favour with the Celtic fanbase.

The 'Lisbon Star' was inconspicuously moved from the crest to the sleeve, but the celtic cross design was resurrected – this time on the back of the shirt, just under the neckline. The thin v-neck made this top appear to some more like a piece of training kit rather than an actual match jersey, and the decision to pair it with white shorts was also criticised by some fans.

Nike would replace Umbro, Celtic's long-term kit suppliers, for the beginning of the 2005/06 season, and they would introduce their own green and silver kit two years later to much better effect.

The 2004 Scottish Cup Final saw Henrik Larsson bag two goals in his farewell match

HOME 2004/05

Match worn by Stanislav Varga

Umbro produced their final Celtic home jersey in time for the start of the 2004/05 season. It was a popular design, but is sadly remembered for a dark day in the club's history.

Sunday 22nd May 2005 was to become known to Celtic supporters as 'Helicopter Sunday', or 'Black Sunday'. For many among the Celtic faithful, this remains their worst-ever day supporting the club as Celtic almost literally threw away the league title in the last two minutes of the season.

Celtic were two points clear of Rangers when they travelled to Motherwell's Fir Park on the final day of the league campaign, safe in the knowledge that all they had to do to be crowned champions was match Rangers' result against Hibernian at Easter Road.

Although Celtic went ahead after 30 minutes through Chris Sutton, the visiting supporters were growing increasingly anxious as news filtered through of a 59th-minute opener for Rangers in Edinburgh. Unthinkably, with just two minutes of the game left to play, Australian striker Scott McDonald equalised for Motherwell. As a shell-shocked Celtic tried to rally, the home side broke away in the dying seconds and McDonald scored again, his deflected shot looping over Rab Douglas in Celtic's goal.

By this time the league trophy had already left Hampden Park in a helicopter – initially setting off in the direction of Fir Park before being dramatically diverted to Edinburgh following McDonald's killer strikes.

The jersey worn on that fateful day had appeared resplendent on its debut the previous August when Celtic unfurled the League Championship flag against the side who would later destroy their title dream. The inclusion of seven green hoops, as seen on this stylish jersey, is always a winning formula and the classic design was complemented by a full-coloured crest, white star and white celtic cross on the back of the neck.

It was a fine way for Umbro to sign-off their tenure, but sadly Martin O'Neill's men had forgotten to read the script.

Defender Stanislav Varga in action during a 2004 Champions League match against Barcelona

SCOTTISH CUP FINAL 2005

Match worn by Chris Sutton

Umbro's final Celtic home jersey was worn for the last time in a competitive match in the 2005 Scottish Cup Final. The afternoon of 28th May 2005 was one of mixed emotions for everyone associated with the club, as while Celtic won the encounter with Dundee United by a solitary Alan Thompson goal, the game marked the end of several distinguished Celtic Park careers.

Martin O'Neill had been a revelation since his Parkhead arrival five years previously, winning seven trophies and leading the club to their third European final, but in May 2005 he had called time on his Celtic tenure and a few days later bowed out with the final winners' medal of his managerial career to date.

Six days earlier Celtic had thrown the league title away at Fir Park, but while surely still reeling from that dismal disappointment they were dogged in their pursuit of silverware against Dundee United.

As well as the end of Celtic's association with Umbro, this Scottish Cup win signalled the end of O'Neill's 'Seville Team', as Rab Douglas, Jackie McNamara, Joos Valgaeren and Paul Lambert all made their final Celtic appearances before joining their talismanic manager in bringing their Hoops careers to a close.

Craig Bellamy also played his last competitive game for the club at Hampden Park that afternoon. The Welshman had the curious habit of modifying his jersey during his short loan stint in Glasgow. The floppy collar (which had a black underside that was often visible when a player was in motion) would always be cut off by the popular striker, who clearly preferred a round-neck shirt.

The match worn edition featured here includes the collar so loathed by Bellamy and was worn in the cup final by Chris Sutton, who missed an 86th-minute penalty – the striker slipping before striking the ball high over Tony Bullock's bar.

The day after the final, the club bade farewell to captain McNamara, whose testimonial match against the Republic of Ireland proved to be the last time Celtic wore an Umbro jersey.

Chris Sutton slips and sends his penalty over the Dundee United bar wearing the cup final jersey featured on these pages (right)

MULTI-COLOURED SWAP SHOP

The incredible Neilly Mochan collection does not just include Celtic jerseys, it also contains historic match worn shirts swapped with some of the club's most illustrious European opponents

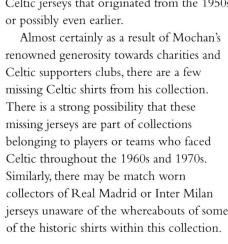

Billy McNeill and Alfredo Di Stéfano shake hands before the Real Madrid legend's testimonial when – unusually – the home side wore blue shorts

"Mochan would hoard old Celtic kit so that he had jerseys to exchange with opponents from all over the globe"

Being bestowed with the honour of accessing the football vault of Neilly Mochan was the inspiration for the compilation of this book, and sorting through Mochan's vast collection (believed to be the largest Celtic-related match worn jersey collection in the world) revealed a truly astonishing wealth of jerseys from other teams.

As many kitmen do, Mochan had a tradition of swapping jerseys with his opposition counterpart. Often the players weren't allowed to swap their own shirts, but the scrupulous Mochan would hoard old Celtic kit so that he had jerseys to exchange with opponents from all over the globe. There is no doubt that during the 1960s kitmen from European clubs were given Celtic jerseys that originated from the 1950s or possibly even earlier.

Almost certainly as a result of Mochan's renowned generosity towards charities and Celtic supporters clubs, there are a few missing Celtic shirts from his collection. There is a strong possibility that these missing jerseys are part of collections belonging to players or teams who faced Celtic throughout the 1960s and 1970s. Similarly, there may be match worn collectors of Real Madrid or Inter Milan jerseys unaware of the whereabouts of some of the historic shirts within this collection.

From literally hundreds of examples of other teams' jerseys, what follows represents a handpicked selection of shirts from the sixties, seventies and eighties that provide a tiny flavour of the 'alternative' Neilly Mochan collection.

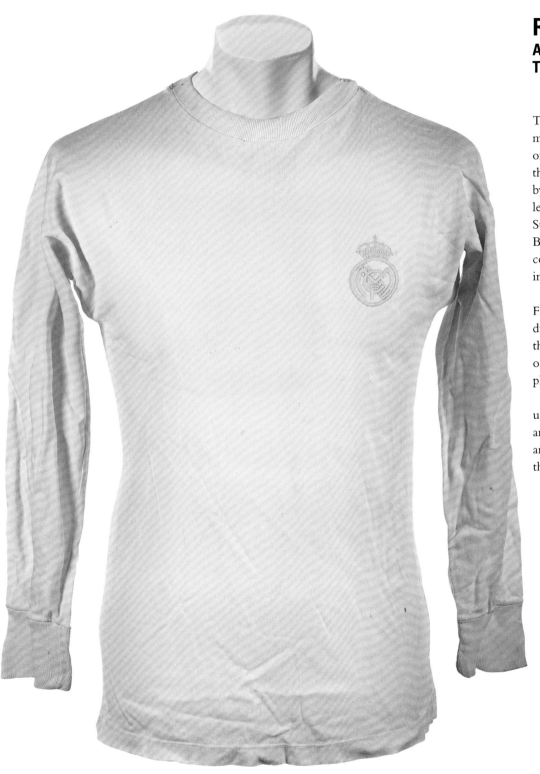

REAL MADRID
ALFREDO DI STÉFANO
TESTIMONIAL, 1967

The iconic all-white Real Madrid kit was made famous by its appearance in eight of the first 11 European Cup Finals, but the Spanish giants were also impressed by Celtic's style – so much so that the legendary Alfredo Di Stéfano invited Jock Stein's European champions to the Santiago Bernabeu Stadium on 7th June 1967 to compete for the Alfredo Di Stéfano Trophy in front of a crowd of more than 120,000.

Celtic's Lisbon Lions (albeit with John Fallon replacing Ronnie Simpson in goal) duly obliged, with Jimmy Johnstone running the show and Bobby Lennox scoring the only goal, and another one-off trophy was placed in the Celtic Park cabinet.

To avoid a clash of colours, Real Madrid unusually broke with tradition in this match and wore blue shorts with their white shirts and socks after Celtic refused to tinker with their own classic strip.

FIORENTINA
EUROPEAN CUP, 1970

Match worn by Giuseppe Longoni

The run to the final of the European Cup in 1970 is often cited as being a trickier route than that negotiated by Celtic in 1966/67. Having progressed against Basel of Switzerland, Celtic dispatched Benfica before facing Italian champions Fiorentina. Originating from Florence – one of the world's fashion capitals – it is no surprise that Fiorentina's jerseys are stylishly sumptuous affairs. However, this unique colour choice actually came about by accident in 1929 when the club's original half-red and half-white shirts ran in the wash to create an eye-catching shade of purple, which was then adopted as the first-choice colour. Fiorentina certainly looked the part when they visited Celtic Park on 4th March 1970, but the home side turned on the style to earn a 3-0 cushion for the second leg.

FEYENOORD
FRIENDLY, 1981

Match worn by Willem van Hanegem

This jersey evokes painful memories of the 1970 European Cup Final defeat at the hands of Feyenoord, who became the first Dutch side to win the tournament when they defeated Jock Stein's men 2-1 after extra-time. However, the Feyenoord shirt worn in the San Siro for that match featured a manufacturer's logo on the left breast. The jersey pictured here was manufactured by English brand Bukta and was worn by Dutch international Willem van Hanegem during a friendly in Rotterdam on 31st July 1981.

AJAX
EUROPEAN CUP, 1982
Match worn by Marco van Basten

This instantly recognisable 1982 Ajax home
jersey is as near perfect as a football shirt can
ever aspire to be. Le Coq Sportif were still
using the v-insert collars made famous in the
seventies, but they certainly didn't look out
of place on this classic strip. Celtic travelled
to play Ajax in the Olympic Stadium (the
tie was moved from De Meer Stadion on
account of the huge crowd), having drawn
the first leg 2-2 at Celtic Park. On a famous
night in Amsterdam, Celtic overcame an
Ajax side featuring such greats as Johan
Cruyff and Wim Kieft 2-1 thanks to goals
from George McCluskey and Charlie
Nicholas. This particular jersey was worn by
a young player who would go on to become
one of the greatest strikers in world football
– Marco van Basten.

SPORTING LISBON
UEFA CUP, 1983

It is not often that Celtic are required to wear their away jerseys at home these days and it is even less likely that their opponents will be wearing green and white hoops. However, that was the case on 2nd November 1983 when Sporting Lisbon were the visitors to Celtic Park in the UEFA Cup. Wearing their lime-green away kit – which later became synonymous with the dramatic clinching of the league title at Love Street in 1986 – Davie Hay's men emphatically overcame a two-goal deficit from the first leg to sweep away their Portuguese opponents 5-0. Future Celtic manager Jozef Vengloš was in charge of this Sporting Lisbon side, who were wearing yet another vintage Le Coq Sportif jersey.

LIVERPOOL
TOMMY BURNS TESTIMONIAL, 1987

Tommy Burns was one of three Celts who were honoured with testimonials in 1987 – Roy Aitken's game was against Manchester United, Davie Provan's was versus Nottingham Forest, and Tommy Burns' match was against Liverpool. An average of more than 40,000 fans attended these matches to ensure that the trio of club stalwarts were amply rewarded, and Kenny Dalglish turned up to two of them (he was a guest for Celtic in the Davie Provan match). The stylish Liverpool side that 'King Kenny' brought up to Celtic Park for Burns' big day went on to win the English First Division title. This featured jersey was match worn by John Aldridge and included the much-missed adidas Trefoil logo.

RAPID VIENNA
EUROPEAN CUP WINNERS' CUP, 1984
Match worn by Rudi Weinhofer

Celtic faced Rapid Vienna three times in 1984. In the first leg of the European Cup Winners' Cup second round match in Austria, the home side wore green-and-white-striped shirts as they comfortably turned Celtic over 3-1. In the return leg at Celtic Park, Davie Hay's men recorded a 3-0 victory that ultimately became infamous. Twelve minutes before full-time a bottle was thrown onto the pitch from the home crowd. It missed everyone but Austrian midfielder Rudi Weinhofer – wearing the very shirt pictured here – collapsed as if he had been poleaxed. It was an opportunistic display of play-acting, but it fooled UEFA into ordering a third encounter at Old Trafford. This time, Rapid Vienna wore red and won the match 1-0 to progress to the quarter-finals. The blue jersey they wore at Parkhead is synonymous with deceit among Celtic fans, which is a shame because it is an enduring adidas classic.

CHAPTER SEVEN

TEN YEARS OF THE SWOOSH

NIKE 2005-15

HOME 2005-07

Match worn by Stiliyan Petrov

Umbro's £25 million, five-year kit deal with Celtic expired in July 2005. The 'double diamond' logo had become synonymous with Celtic's green and white hoops – indeed Umbro had been the only ever commercial manufacturer of Celtic's jerseys – until American sportswear giants Nike signed what the club described as "the largest commercial licensing transaction entered into by Celtic".

The famous 'swoosh' would complement what Nike recognised as the global appeal of the Celtic brand, just in time for the beginning of Gordon Strachan's Parkhead reign.

Nike's first home kit was launched by the club's captain – the combative Neil Lennon – with the official marketing campaign, referring to him as a '21st Century Bhoy', a reference to the manufacturer's groundbreaking technology meeting "a century of Celtic tradition".

The new jersey represented a promising start for Nike. The design incorporated six untarnished green hoops, the full-colour crest and star were located in the centre of the shirt and the collar was a thin round-neck. The hoops on the sleeves extended to the neck, with thin white panels breaking them up at the top of the chest.

Nike's first Celtic shirt made its competitive debut at the same venue where Martin O'Neill's title hopes had been shattered the previous season – Fir Park. Future Celt Scott McDonald equalised John Hartson's first-half hat-trick on the hour mark, before Motherwell went 4-3 up with just six minutes remaining, only for substitute Craig Beattie to dramatically spare Strachan's blushes with a last-minute equaliser.

Performances soon vastly improved as Strachan put his own mark on the team with the introduction of Polish goalkeeper Artur Boruc and Japanese playmaker Shunsuke Nakamura. By the season's conclusion, Celtic had won the league and League Cup double.

Above: Stiliyan Petrov brought a wealth of creativity to the Celtic midfield when he joined the club from CSKA Sofia in 1999

Right: A Coors Light-sponsored version of Nike's home jersey was worn during the pre-season tour to the US in 2006

AWAY 2005/06

Match worn by Stephen McManus

The 2005/06 season – Gordon Strachan's first in charge at the club – was notable for the tale of two Nike change jerseys and the memories they ingrained in the minds of Celtic fans.

First up was the all-green kit, a colour combination that Celtic hadn't used for a full away outfit since 1966/67. The popular 1978 and 1982 jerseys had employed a similar tone of green, but this latest effort used it on the shirt, shorts and socks. The white v-neck collar was thin and extended to flashes of white on the sleeves. The Lisbon Star (above a centred crest) was embroidered in yellow, as was the Nike swoosh to match the squad name and numbering to the rear.

While the design itself was not unpopular, this jersey's reputation will forever be tarnished by the fact that it was worn in two of the club's most embarrassing results of recent times. The 5-0 humiliation at the hands of Slovakia's Artmedia Bratislava in the second qualifying round of the Champions League was, at the time, the worst European result in Celtic's history.

The second shameful performance featuring the all-green kit came in what was Roy Keane's debut for the club, and also saw the introduction of unfortunate Chinese defender Du Wei. Holders Celtic travelled to Broadwood where they faced lower-league Clyde on 8th January 2006 in the Scottish Cup. It was an afternoon of abject despair for Strachan's stuttering Celts. Unthinkably, Clyde – who were co-managed by Celtic's 1989 Scottish Cup hero Joe Miller – won 2-1, had two goals disallowed and missed a penalty, while Du was subbed off at half-time after a disastrous showing.

To his credit, Gordon Strachan turned it around in his maiden campaign at Celtic Park and went on to secure both the league title and League Cup.

Stephen McManus in the all-green Nike change kit forever tarnished by two terrible results

THIRD 2005-07

Match prepared for Shunsuke Nakamura

If the all-green away kit of 2005/06 saw the worst of times, then the black alternative jersey was the complete opposite.

If ever there was a kit template that was transformed by a simple change of colour then this was undoubtedly it. Whereas the all-green strip looked rather bland to some, this all-black ensemble oozed class – as did Japanese midfield genius Shunsuke Nakamura, who joined Celtic in July 2005. With the faintest hint of green on the v-neck collar and a similar section of green on the socks, this was yet another kit which benefited from a 'less is more' approach.

Unlike its green counterpart, this kit was criminally underworn by Gordon Strachan's side. It made a welcome appearance at Easter Road for the league match against Hibernian on 18th September 2005, when Nakamura – wearing short sleeves – threaded a pass through to Stiliyan Petrov for a fifth-minute opener that sealed a tight encounter. It is possible that the jersey pictured opposite was the Japanese icon's long-sleeved option prepared for this match.

As Celtic's new kit manufacturers, Nike had wasted little time in employing the colour black into their armoury. Nowadays, with replica kit sales accounting for a large proportion of clubs' merchandising revenue, considerable thought is given to the colour and design of the alternative strips not just from a sporting perspective but in terms of their suitability as items of leisurewear. With black recognised worldwide as a highly fashionable colour, it has become a popular away kit choice for numerous manufacturers.

Black is also relatively new to the colour palette available to kit designers since up until the mid 1990s it was invariably the exclusive preserve of the referee and match officials.

Shunsuke Nakamura gets on the ball wearing the short-sleeved version of this jersey

AWAY 2006-08

Match worn by Mark Wilson

Nike produced a modern classic with the away jersey unveiled before the beginning of the 2006/07 season. The black-and-green-striped shirt drew inspiration from the change shirt of 1973, which Jock Stein so despised and which was worn against a Bobby Charlton-inspired Preston North End in a friendly match on 2nd August 1974.

The new shirt worked well with black shorts and socks as Nike kept the whole ensemble simple to great effect. A black button-up collar, white star and Nike swoosh completed the look, along with another white star and '1888' below the neck on the rear.

The jersey featured on these pages was worn by Celtic right-back Mark Wilson during a friendly match against Chelsea at Stamford Bridge on 9th August 2006. A team of Chelsea all-stars, managed by Celtic's old foe José Mourinho, went behind to Gary Caldwell's opener before Shaun Wright-Phillips equalised for the home side on the stroke of half-time. This 1-1 draw was the first time this kit saw action, but it did make some more memorable appearances as the 2006/07 season progressed to a tantalising climax.

During Celtic's Champions League campaign, they wore this change kit in the away legs of the ties against Manchester United, Benfica and FC Copenhagen. For the first time in the club's history, Celtic advanced beyond the group stages of European football's revamped premier competition, and they were only knocked out by eventual winners AC Milan after a dramatic extra-time winner by Kaká in the San Siro.

The player who is instantly associated with this jersey is Japanese genius Shunsuke Nakamura, on account of two unforgettable goals the Yokohama-born playmaker scored while wearing it. The first was one of two free-kicks against Manchester United in the Champions League, when he bent a 25-yard effort beyond a stranded Edwin van der Sar to level the score at 2-2. Seven months later, Nakamura scored an injury-time winner from a similar distance against Kilmarnock at Rugby Park to clinch the league title.

Defender Mark Wilson lines up ahead of the Champions League clash with Manchester United in September 2006

EUROPE 2006-08

Match worn by Stephen McManus

Nike produced three separate kits for Celtic in the first year of their partnership and labclled them as 'home', 'away' and 'third' strips. Two more outfits were released the following season – with the home jersey being retained for a second campaign – but the two new additions were nominated as the 'away' and 'European' kits.

Celtic's new kit manufacturers returned to 1968/69 for inspiration when designing this all-white European kit. Like Jimmy 'Jinky' Johnston's favourite Celtic kit from his playing days (on account of his fond memories of playing against Real Madrid in the Alfredo Di Stéfano testimonial played in the Bernabeu Stadium in 1967), this updated version included some subtle flashes of colour.

A green and yellow stripe ran from the top to the bottom of this jersey, running beneath the full-colour four-leaf clover crest. The embroidered badge was set below a black star to signify the club's 1967 European Cup win. There was also another flash of green and yellow on the sleeve of what was a striking and popular design.

Although officially designated the European strip, the white kit was regularly used in domestic competition while the black-and-green-striped jersey actually saw plenty of Champions League action. When playing in white against Dunfermline at East End Park, Celtic opted to wear black shorts and socks as an alternative to the original white versions more commonly seen.

This design first appeared in a pre-season friendly on 12th July 2006 against MLS side DC United, in what was the Washington club's 10th anniversary season. Gordon Strachan's Celtic suffered their third close-season defeat in a row as they prepared for their defence of the Scottish league and League Cup. During this game Celtic wore the 'Coors Light' logos across their jerseys which was more familiar to the club's US fanbase than the usual Carling branding.

When sold as a replica, this jersey was available to purchase without a sponsor, a trend that has become popular with the Celtic supporters.

Above: Stephen McManus in action in a friendly against Everton in July 2006

Right: Once again the Carling sponsor logo was replaced with Coors Light for the pre-season tour to the US

HOME 2007/08

Match worn by Lee Naylor

If there was a sure-fire way for Nike to further ingratiate themselves with the Celtic fanbase, then it was to release a home kit that paid homage to the club's finest football team – the Lisbon Lions. That is exactly what the kit manufacturer did for the 2007/08 season, with the result being one of the best-loved kits in Celtic's history.

As part of the 40th anniversary celebrations of Celtic's European Cup win, Nike ran a 'Still as Fierce' advertising campaign, which showed Celts from the 2007 squad in mirrored poses alongside their 1967 counterparts.

The jersey itself was a modern interpretation of the strip worn in Lisbon, with six untarnished green hoops complemented by a white round-neck. The attention to detail by Nike was particularly impressive. The crests, both on the jersey and the shorts, were surrounded by gold embroidered letters which read *"25 Maio 1967 – Leões de Lisboa – 40° Aniversario"* to commemorate the club's famous triumph in Portugal.

This detail did not, however, appear on the version of the jersey worn by Celtic in the Champions League, as can be seen on the Lee Naylor jersey pictured opposite which was worn in Europe's premier competition. This is because of strict UEFA rules surrounding club crests and additional messaging.

On the domestically-worn jerseys there was also a small patch at the bottom which read: "For it's a grand old team to play for. The Tunnel. Estádio Nacional. 25th May 1967." This was a reference to the war-cry of Bertie Auld, who started singing the Hoops' anthem as Celtic and Inter Milan stood in the tunnel before the game. Inter – bemused and unnerved – were psychologically defeated before they even stepped onto the pitch.

One feature of this 40th anniversary jersey that was much improved from its Lisbon original was its advanced technical specification. The shirt was made from Nike Sphere Dry material, a lightweight fabric designed for maximum player comfort which had been developed for the previous year's World Cup kits.

Above: Lee Naylor is pictured in the Champions League version of this popular jersey against Benfica

Right: A commemorative crest appeared on the domestic version of this celebrated jersey

AWAY 2007/08

Match prepared for Steven Pressley

Nike continued their excellent run of form with the 2007/08 away jersey, which was yet another inspired design. It was clear that their designers were dipping into the Celtic jersey archive, as this kit owed an obvious debt to Umbro's green and silver effort of 2004/05, which brought to mind the Pablo Picasso aphorism – "Good artists copy; great artists steal."

The result was yet another Nike masterclass in the art of understatement. The silver round-neck matched the crest, star and swoosh details, which all complemented the main body of dark green. There was also additional detail added to the four-leaf clover crest in celebration of the 40th anniversary of the Lisbon triumph.

Although this commemorative crest was present on this jersey during its first appearance (a pre-season friendly against Peterborough on 13th July 2007) and in domestic games as Celtic went on to claim their third consecutive league championship title, it is absent from the shirt featured here. Due to UEFA rules, the additional embroidery was not included on the jerseys worn in the away ties in the Champions League throughout this campaign – against Spartak Moscow (a 1-1 draw), Benfica (a narrow 1-0 loss) and AC Milan (a further 1-0 defeat).

The featured jersey was prepared for central defender Steven Pressley for the single-goal defeat to AC Milan in the San Siro on 4th December 2007. Celtic wore the strip with white socks that night, even though there was no colour clash with their Italian opponents' black ones.

Gordon Strachan once again led the Scottish champions through the Champions League group stages and into the last 16 of the tournament, where they were overcome 4-2 on aggregate by the mighty Barcelona.

Steven Pressley on the ball
in the San Siro v AC Milan

HOME 2008-10

Match worn by Scott McDonald

Nike's first two Celtic home jerseys had been relatively traditional designs, but they pushed the boundaries further with their third effort for the beginning of the 2008/09 season. Although this was still a fairly clean and uncomplicated jersey, the introduction of yellow to the home strip was breaking new ground.

Again, the green hoops were untarnished and six-fold, the full-colour crest was embroidered on the left breast with a yellow star above it, the swoosh was embroidered in yellow on green, and the v-neck and sleeves also had yellow trims. The shorts and socks continued the yellow trim theme, with the tops of the stockings including green bands for the first time in almost a decade.

Continuing the theme of including historical detail seen on the previous home jersey, this shirt included a Willie Maley quote on the inside collar, which read, "It's not the creed nor nationality that counts. It's the man himself." Maley, a former player, had been Celtic's first manager and served in that position with distinction for some 43 years. The quote had been his mantra, and that of the club, in terms of being an inclusive club open to all.

Despite being undefeated in all three home games, Celtic were knocked out of the Champions League – the competition in which the featured jersey was worn – at the group stages having failed to win once on their travels.

The disappointment of being out of Europe before Christmas was softened somewhat by a 1-0 victory at Ibrox on 27th December 2008, which put Celtic seven points clear of Rangers at the league's summit. Few would have argued at the turn of the year that Gordon Strachan's men were on their way to winning their fourth title in a row, but losing the final Old Firm encounter of the year was followed by Celtic winning just one of their final three league games as they gave up their league crown with a whimper.

Above: Scott McDonald celebrates scoring at Ibrox alongside teammates Scott Brown and Shunsuke Nakamura

Right: On 8th November 2008 v Motherwell, for the first time the Celtic jersey – like those of all SPL teams – carried a poppy emblem to mark Remembrance Sunday

AWAY 2008/09

Match worn by Cillian Sheridan

Having already successfully delved into the 'best of' section of Celtic's back catalogue with the revamped all-black, all-white, green and silver, and green and black kit designs, Nike's next attempt at bringing a classic design back to life worked flawlessly. Canary yellow top, green shorts and yellow socks – in the world of Celtic away jerseys this colour scheme is a match made in heaven.

Umbro had introduced the colourway in 1973 and returned to it another half-a-dozen times over the next 30 years. It is safe to say that most Celtic supporters would consider yellow to be the club's traditional away colour, so it made sense to reintroduce what had (apart from the radical 1989 design) been universally popular with the traditional fanbase.

The yellow body of the 2008/09 away jersey was almost completely untarnished (other than the Carling sponsor logo), with only the back half of the round-neck collar and the sleeve trim in green. The Nike swoosh embroidery and star above the four-leaf clover crest were also green, and crucially – like the classic centenary away shirt – the badge was embroidered in full colour.

This kit made its first appearance on 18th July 2008 in Southampton's testimonial for their Norwegian defender Claus Lundekvam. It also featured on the road in the Champions League against Manchester United and Aalborg. Republic of Ireland international Cillian Sheridan appeared as a substitute in both of these games, and the featured European-spec shirt was worn in one of these encounters.

An alternative version of the strip (with a bespoke set of yellow shorts) was worn against Hibernian at Easter Road on 7th December 2008 and 17th May 2009. Although the all-yellow kit was also pleasing on the eye, the original version with green shorts has become an undoubted classic.

Cillian Sheridan in the classic combination of canary yellow jersey and green shorts

EUROPE 2009/10

Match worn by Georgios Samaras

This was yet another 'European' kit that was destined never to be worn in European competition, but the understated look with a hint of Celtic tartan nevertheless became another instant classic.

On 31st May 2009, Celtic paid tribute to their much-loved ex-player and manager Tommy Burns, who had passed away a year earlier after a brave battle against cancer. A benefit match was arranged at Parkhead between Celtic's first team and a club legends XI, with the first team turning out in this new kit.

The crisp white top had a simple v-neck, a green embroidered Nike swoosh and star and a full-colour crest. A single strip of Celtic tartan adorned each shoulder from collar to sleeve. The use of tartan extended to the shorts, which worked better than many fans might have feared. The kit was finished off with white socks which featured a single green hoop.

The use of tartan in football kits was not a new phenomenon. Dundee had worn it back in 1953 for an anniversary tour; manufacturers Matchwinner had adopted the pattern for Greenock Morton's blue home and red away strips in the early 1990s; and the Scottish national side had Umbro to thank for their classic 1994-96 home design.

A more obvious (and perhaps less aesthetically pleasing) use of tartan in Celtic jerseys later appeared in Nike's final season as the club's kit manufacturers in 2014/15, but this original example is regarded by many as their vintage release.

The 'Celtic Tartan Collection' had long been a merchandising line from the club's commercial team. This was used for popular garments such as scarves and blankets (often required in the Scottish winter months), but it also extended to ties, kilts and bunnets, which were popular during the Fergus McCann era (the Celtic saviour often wore a grey bunnet and thus became affectionately known by Celtic supporters as 'The Bunnet').

Striker Georgios Samaras in action against Hearts in the SPL, despite this being Celtic's designated 'European' change jersey

AWAY 2009-11

Match worn by Stephen McManus

Nike continued to reprise popular Celtic designs from days gone by, and the potential resurrection of the 1990s 'Bumblebee' shirt had garnered some traction on social media and online forums amongst fans whose memories of the original were probably skewed by their fondness for some of the players who made their name in it. Extravagant and oversized, the original jersey was certainly of its time and the 'Three Amigos' who briefly wore it (Paolo Di Canio, Jorge Cadete and Pierre van Hooijdonk) had gained as much of a cult status as the shirt itself over subsequent years.

Rumours that Nike were about to launch an updated Bumblebee kit for the 2009/10 season began to surface online when an image appeared of a fan wearing the neon yellow and black hoops. This turned out to be the real deal and Celtic later ran a marketing campaign based on the much-loved phrase, often used by 1980s midfield maestro Paul McStay, about the club, "There's a buzz about the place."

The modern take on the classic design was certainly more refined than the original. There were five black and five yellow equal-width hoops and a simple black round-neck collar. The Nike swoosh and club crest were yellow on black while the star above it was black on yellow. The strip was completed by black shorts with yellow trim, and black-and-yellow-hooped socks.

First worn during Celtic's successful Wembley Cup appearance during the 2009/10 pre-season, the Bumblebee's later excursions were less memorable, with the strip being worn in defeats to Arsenal in the Champions League, Hapoel Tel Aviv in the Europa League, and a 4-0 league reverse at the hands of St Mirren, which signalled the end of Tony Mowbray's time in charge at Celtic Park. This kit also appeared with the Tennent's sponsor's logo the following season.

The featured jersey was worn by Stephen McManus in the Europa League, either against Hapoel Tel Aviv on 17th September 2009 or when he was an unused substitute against Hamburg on 5th November 2009.

Stephen McManus, pictured during the 2009 clash with St Mirren

HOME 2010-2012

Match worn by Georgios Samaras

With three home jerseys in five years all receiving largely positive reviews, Nike had been on a fine run since winning Celtic's long-term contract from Umbro back in 2005. However, for a certain section of fans the bubble burst with their fourth set of hoops.

The six green hoops of this jersey incorporated a diagonal pattern with multiple repetitions of the year '1888'. This type of detail – presumably included as a reminder to any Celtic fan who was unaware that the club played their first game in the May of that year – was in marked contrast to the subtlety of Nike's previous efforts. In addition, 'Celtic' appeared in black uppercase letters on the back of the shirt underneath the collar. The refreshing flashes of yellow found on the previous home kit were replaced with black, and the collar was a v-necked/winged hybrid. For purists, the whole composition was not assisted by the new sponsor – Tennent's – being pasted accross two hoops.

While the new kit was a little uneasy on the eye, the Celtic faithful were hopeful that Neil Lennon's new-look side would fare better on the field of play. The jersey was introduced during Celtic's typical glut of pre-season friendlies, before making its competitive debut in the home tie of the third qualifying round of the Champions League against Braga of Portugal. Although Celtic recorded a 2-1 victory on the night, they sadly failed to progress by virtue of their 3-0 loss in the first leg.

Another bite of the European cherry was presented to Lennon's men in the form of a Europa League qualifier against Utrecht of the Netherlands, but Celtic failed to impress as they were again beaten 4-2 over the two legs.

The shirt featured opposite was worn by Georgios Samaras against Motherwell on 22nd April 2012 and features the Greek striker's name in Thai script. Later the jerseys were auctioned off to raise funds for the 'Thai Tims' supporters club.

Greek striker Georgios Samaras scored 74 times for Celtic in all competitions

AWAY 2010/11

Match worn by Paddy McCourt

Buoyed by the success of their design throwbacks, Nike attempted to recreate the spirit of Love Street 1986 with this lime green change kit for the 2010/11 campaign. The 'Bumblebee' jersey had been a popular enough release, but it had perhaps not been enjoyed to the same extent as the original. Similarly, the beauty of the 1986 away design was in its simplicity, and it was a tall order for the updated version to live up to the heights of the much-loved original.

Had Nike remained true to the original and used dark green instead of black for the trim, this design may have been more popular. In addition to the lime green and black colourway, the Nike swoosh and star above the crest were embroidered in bright yellow, whilst the logo of new sponsors Tennent's appeared in red on the shorts, which resulted in a rather convoluted design.

This jersey debuted on the opening day of the domestic league campaign against Inverness Caledonian Thistle on 14th August 2010, an encounter won by a single Paddy McCourt goal. When Celtic faced St Mirren in Paisley three months later wearing this kit, they did so sporting lime shorts. However, the supporters were more interested in a different, more controversial addition to this new outfit.

The St Mirren game took place on 14th November 2010 – Remembrance Sunday – and Celtic (like all Scottish and English top-flight clubs since 2008) had agreed to wear an embroidered poppy on the centre of the shirt's chest, but it was to be the final time they did so.

Banners which read, "Your deeds would shame all the devils in hell" and, "No blood-stained poppy on our hoops" had been unfurled at the previous week's league match against Aberdeen by Celtic's ultra fan group, The Green Brigade, who subsequently boycotted the St Mirren clash and stated that their opposition to the wearing of the poppy was on account of acts by the British Army during the conflict in Ireland (including 'Bloody Sunday') as well as civilian casualties inflicted by them in Iraq and Afghanistan.

Following the fan protests, Celtic did not wear the poppy on their jerseys again.

Paddy McCourt surges forward during Celtic's clash with St Mirren in November 2010, when the Celtic jersey featured a poppy for the final time

SCOTTISH CUP FINAL 2011

Match worn by Mark Wilson

No doubt the 2010-12 home jersey will always be held in high regard by Neil Lennon, for it was while wearing this kit that Celtic won his first managerial silverware in the form of the 2011 Scottish Cup. The following year, still wearing this strip, the club went on to lift its first league title under the Northern Irishman's stewardship.

The first of these triumphs took place at the unpopular national stadium under a constant stream of torrential rain as Lennon's men overcame Motherwell with relative ease. Celtic's three goals came from South Korean midfielder Ki Sung-yueng, utility man Charlie Mulgrew and an own goal from Motherwell's Stephen Craigan.

Accompanying this cup final jersey were white shorts and socks. The shorts included a green design down each side, and the sponsor's logo also appeared on them for the first time. The red Tennent's 'T' was unusually situated above the Celtic crest in a commercial trend that would continue for six years.

Whilst every trophy success should be savoured, this season promised so much more than a solitary cup. In fact, for a lengthy period of the campaign it genuinely looked as though Lennon could win a treble in his first full season in charge at Celtic Park. However, the League Cup Final was lost in extra-time to Rangers, while the league challenge was surrendered in Inverness when the Highlanders shocked the Hoops with a 3-2 defeat. Rangers clinched the title by a single point as Georgios Samaras was left to rue a late penalty miss at Ibrox at the end of April with the match scoreless.

A soggy Mark Wilson plays
the ball during the rain-soaked
2011 Scottish Cup Final

AWAY 2011/12

Match worn by Anthony Stokes

During their tenure as Celtic's kit manufacturer, Nike went through a series of away shirts inspired by Celtic's classic hoops. Even the lime green jersey of the previous season had subtle hoops within the background pattern. The grey and white jersey released for the 2011/12 season executed this design strategy particularly well.

The shirt featured horizontal green pinstripes that separated each grey and white hoop, and the same green was used on the round-neck collar and sleeves. The four leaf clover crest was embroidered in full colour, and the Nike swoosh and star were black (as was the 'Celtic' detail underneath the neck to the rear). There was a further '1888' detail on the sleeve of this shirt.

Two features of the Tennent's sponsorship throughout their partnership with the club that were particularly unpopular with traditionalists were the fact that the main shirt logo was positioned too high up on the jersey – which meant that it broke two hoops, rather than sitting within a singular hoop – as well as the presence of the red 'T' logo on the shorts, which looked out of place with this colour scheme. For some, these two commercial inclusions marred an otherwise vintage design of the modern age.

This jersey was first worn at Pittodrie, with its regular green shorts and white socks with green trim, in the league fixture on 7th August 2011. This was strictly unnecessary as there was no clash with Celtic's home kit, but with three strips to give an airing the club had begun to regularly play in change kits against Aberdeen and Hearts.

Celtic's goal in the 1-0 victory over Aberdeen that day was scored by Republic of Ireland international Anthony Stokes, whose 2012 League Cup Final jersey is the featured example here. Sadly Celtic lost this match 1-0 to Kilmarnock.

This cup final jersey includes the tournament sponsor's sleeve patches, as well as the match detail between the Celtic crest and Nike logo. A minor disappointment for match worn collecting aficionados is that the fact that the match detail is heat pressed rather than embroidered onto the jersey.

Anthony Stokes claims the match ball after scoring a hat-trick against Peterhead in the fourth round of the League Cup

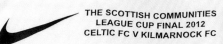

THE SCOTTISH COMMUNITIES
LEAGUE CUP FINAL 2012
CELTIC FC V KILMARNOCK FC

TENNENT'S

STOKES

10

THIRD 2011/12

Match worn by Ki Sung-yueng

Although this was billed as a 'third' kit by Nike, it was far more regularly worn by Celtic than its grey and white 'away' counterpart. In the modern age, some releases seem to be designed in such a way to appeal to younger members of the club's fanbase, and this strip appeared to fall into that category.

Nike returned to the yellow and black colour scheme of the 'Bumblebee' kit, although the yellow used here was a deeper, less luminous tone. Hoops featured once again, although these particular ones were divided up into four quarters of alternating thickness. A black round-neck collar and yellow sleeves completed the design, which included a full-colour embroidered four-leaf clover crest with gold star above, and a white Nike swoosh. The shorts were black with yellow detail, and the socks were yellow with a black band at the top.

This kit was worn for the first competitive match of the 2011/12 season when Celtic travelled to Easter Road to face Hibernian on 24th July 2011 – a match that kicked off Celtic's historic run of nine consecutive league title wins between 2012 to 2019. A 2-0 victory was secured courtesy of goals from Republic of Ireland international Anthony Stokes and South Korea's Ki Sung-yueng.

A more pivotal match in which this kit was worn came in a league encounter at Rugby Park on 15th October 2011. Celtic were three goals down to Kilmarnock at half-time, and Neil Lennon has since admitted that he feared for his job during the interval. A memorable second-half comeback, however, resulted in three goals in the last 17 minutes to save Celtic's – and Lennon's – season.

Ki Sung-yueng celebrates scoring against Hibs at Easter Road, the match in which this jersey made its competitive debut

HOME 2012/13

125th ANNIVERSARY

Match worn by Kris Commons

Another fairytale chapter was written in the history of this unique football club on 7th November 2012 when the unfancied champions of Scotland defeated Barcelona – then the greatest club side in the world – to celebrate the Glasgow underdog's 125th birthday.

As the Green Brigade turned Celtic Park into a green and white fortress to the backdrop of *Zadok The Priest*, no one gave the home side a modicum of hope against a team which had not lost an away match in the Champions League for six years.

Teenager Tony Watt made his entrance on 72 minutes of this famous match, replacing Mikael Lustig, with Celtic a goal up virtue of a Victor Wanyama header. Just 11 minutes later, a Fraser Forster clearance was misjudged by Xavi 10 yards inside his own half. Watt timed his run to perfection, took one touch and bulleted his shot beyond Victor Valdes.

The day before this monumental victory, Celtic had celebrated their 125th anniversary, and a silver/grey celtic knot-work pattern had been added to the crest on the home jersey released at the start of the season to commemorate this landmark.

The new Nike jersey featured nine green hoops – significantly, since Celtic were embarking on their first defence of the league title in a winning sequence that would subsequently equal their own record of 'nine-in-a-row'.

Another notable departure was the positioning of the Tennent's logo, which was much smaller than usual and subtly positioned beneath the Celtic crest, creating a clean and classic look in keeping with the anniversary celebrations. The overall design is undoubtedly one of Celtic's most popular in recent years.

The accompanying shorts were white (again with the red 'T' of sponsor Tennent's), but for the first time since the 1930s Celtic wore black socks with their home kit, topped off with green and white hoops. The black socks made an appearance for the league opener against Aberdeen but were quickly consigned to the kit hamper and replaced with the more familiar white.

Kris Commons in action wearing the 125th anniversary kit, with white socks rather than black

AWAY 2012/13

125th ANNIVERSARY

Match worn by Joe Ledley

Nike raised the bar with all three kits for Celtic's 2012/13 campaign – a season in which Celtic celebrated their 125th birthday in style.

The contemporary away kit was comprised of a two-tone black-hooped top, black shorts and black socks. The jersey also included green, white and yellow details to the sleeves (which was repeated on the socks) to reflect Celtic's Irish heritage, whilst the club crest was surrounded by a grey circular celtic-knot pattern with the European Cup star above it and the dates '1888-2013' underneath.

The black strip was first used on 21st July 2012 against Ajax in a pre-season 4-0 friendly defeat. The sleeve and sock tricolour detail had been a striking feature of the promotional launch images, but these details could both be folded inwards to make the kit appear completely black, which was how it looked by the time Celtic travelled to Finland to face HJK Helsinki in the Champions League qualifying round the following month.

The envy of all the match worn shirt connoisseurs would be the version of this jersey that was worn in Russia against Spartak Moscow in the Champions League, when Celtic wore a sponsorless edition of this modern classic. Then, having progressed to the last 16 of the competition, Celtic wore another one-off version of the jersey – with 'Tennent's Extra' in place as the sponsor's logo – for the 2-0 defeat away to Juventus that saw them exit the tournament.

The featured shirt was worn by Welsh international Joe Ledley at Rugby Park in a 3-1 victory on 8th December 2012. The logo that features on the middle of the jersey's chest is for the Celtic FC Foundation – the club's charitable arm. Following matches when the Foundation's emblem appears on Celtic's jerseys, the shirts are auctioned online for the benefit of various supported charities.

Above: Joe Ledley celebrates scoring in the 2013 Scottish Cup Final, which saw Celtic clinch the double

Left: The Celtic FC Foundation logo sometimes appeared in the centre of this shirt style (right)

THIRD 2012/13

Match worn by Scott Brown

The emotion-stirring video that accompanied the launch of Celtic's commemorative 125th anniversary kit shows the club's manager, Neil Lennon, walking past historic Celtic jerseys before entering the club's boardroom where memorabilia is spread across a polished table. As Billy Connolly narrates, Lennon picks out a photograph of Celtic's first-ever team, a picture which instantly captures the Northern Irishman's imagination. A nod of approval follows before Lennon makes his way into the dressing room to give his players a team-talk, which begins, "If you know the history…"

That sentiment became the tagline of Celtic's marketing campaign for the anniversary season's third strip, which was reminiscent of the club's very first outfit – a white jersey with a black button-up collar, black shorts and black-and-green-hooped socks. The original crest (a celtic cross) was reworked into a green and white modernistic design, and the Nike and Tennent's logos were white-on-white, which added to the classy, untarnished demeanour of the kit.

Celtic's chief executive Peter Lawwell said: "Celtic is looking to add new chapters to their illustrious history and the 125th anniversary kit is a lasting tribute to a long and rich tradition."

Despite its historical inspiration, however, Nike were keen to promote the fact that the jersey was made from their cutting-edge, lightweight Dri-FIT fabric, which was engineered to keep the players dry from sweat whilst withstanding the rigours of the modern footballer.

The only real negative aspect of this kit was the lack of game-time that it enjoyed. Five days after it was unveiled, Celtic wore it at home to Hearts in a league match, with Greek international Georgios Samaras scoring the only goal of the game in the first half.

The featured shirt is likely to have been worn by Scott Brown in the league encounter at Tannadice on 4th November 2012, when, after being 2-0 up with 10 minutes left to play, Dundee United scored two goals in the final two minutes to pull the score level.

Worn so rarely, this jersey is yet another extremely rare and hard to find edition for match worn collectors.

Scott Brown controls the ball against Dundee on Boxing Day 2012, one of the few occasions when this shirt was worn

HOME 2013-15

Match worn by Anthony Stokes

Nike produced five Celtic home jerseys between 2005 and 2013 and had, in the minds of most purists, only got the green and white hoops 'wrong' on one occasion (2010-12). Many of the manufacturer's other kits had become modern favourites and, as the period of their kit deal with the club came to an end, at the beginning of the 2013/14 season they had one final opportunity to further enhance their Celtic legacy.

The home jersey that Nike released for their final two seasons as Celtic's kit manufacturer very nearly attained 'classic' status. The new shirt included many of the hallmarks of the most popular designs of the past: it had a plain white v-neck collar and the full-colour crest on the left breast. However, two aspects of this set of hoops disappointed the aficionados.

The first was the positioning of the new Magners sponsor logo, which once again was not confined to a single hoop – a huge bone of contention among shirt enthusiasts.

Even more sacrilegious was the breaking up of the hoops themselves, with each of the four main hoops divided into seven smaller bands. This was apparently supposed to pay homage to the iconic Celts who wore the famous No.7 shirt – such as Jimmy Johnstone and Henrik Larsson – but some cynical fans felt that it looked more like a commercial nod towards the Magners logo.

The kit served Celtic well, however. Neil Lennon won his third consecutive league title in 2013/14 before he surprisingly stood down as manager. Lennon's replacement, the Norwegian Ronny Deila, won the club's fourth consecutive title in 2014/15 and added the League Cup to complete an impressive double in his debut season.

During the club's Champions League qualifying round play-off tie against Shakhter Karagandy on 20th August 2013, the Magners logo was replaced with Tipperary Natural Mineral Water due to restrictions on alcohol advertising in Kazakhstan.

Above: Irish striker Anthony Stokes lifts the Scottish League Cup in 2015 wearing the jersey featured here

Right: A 'Tipperary' sponsored version of this jersey was worn against Shakhter Karagandy in Kazakhstan

THE SCOTTISH LEAGUE CUP FINAL
PRESENTED BY QTS
15TH MARCH 2015

MAGNERS®

STOKES
10

AWAY 2013/14

Match worn by Kris Commons

Like Nike's 2008/09 away jersey, this effort was another return to the popular yellow and green Celtic change kits that had worked so well back in the eighties.

The bold yellow body of this jersey included seven small green hoops around the middle of the shirt, a nod to the seven sections of each hoop on the home jersey. The collar was a crossover green v-neck, and there were also thin green cuffs on the sleeves. The four-leaf clover crest was a full-coloured embroidered badge, while there was also a green Nike swoosh and black star. Like the outfit of five years previously, it was worn with green shorts and yellow socks (which also featured seven small green hoops). This jersey also bore the logo of the club's new shirt sponsor, Irish cider brand Magners.

On the inside of the back of the neck, the following Sir Robert Kelly quote was printed, "This Celtic Football Club is much more than a football club. To a lot of people, it's a way of life."

Kelly had been a key figure in the history of the Glasgow club. His father, James, had been Celtic's first captain, and thereafter he served on the board until 1931. Robert Kelly became a director in 1932 and he remained on the board until 1971.

The first appearance of this kit came in the legends charity match on 8th September 2013. The benefit game had been arranged for Stiliyan Petrov, who was undergoing treatment for leukaemia, and both sides wore current Celtic strips for the match. Petrov's side (who sported the kit seen here) featured players such as Dimitar Berbatov alongside several celebrities – including comedian John Bishop and rock star James Allan from the band Glasvegas – who possessed a 'Celtic State of Mind'.

The featured long-sleeved jersey was worn by Scottish football's top goalscorer and 2013/14 PFA Scotland Players' Player of the Year, Kris Commons. It includes the Scottish Premiership sleeve patches and names and numbers font.

Kris Commons' creativity and eye for goal made him a popular player during his Celtic career

IRISH FAMINE MEMORIAL SHIRT 2014

Match worn by Mikael Lustig

Since 2009, Celtic have displayed the National Famine Memorial Day logo on their jersey during the third weekend of May every year.

The club have been criticised in certain quarters for the decision to remember the Great Famine (*An Gorta Mór*) in this way, but Celtic and its fans would argue that it is their birthright to commemorate its Irish roots in this respectful way. It could well be a case of those critics simply not knowing their history.

The formation of Celtic Football Club was intrinsically linked to Glasgow's Irish diaspora, who had migrated in huge numbers during the Great Famine which had led to the death by starvation of more than a million Irish men, women and children. A further two million were forced to flee starvation, with many of them migrating to North America and the United Kingdom.

Brother Walfrid, an Irish Marist Brother from County Sligo who had been teaching in Glasgow since the 1870s, founded Celtic Football Club on 6th November 1887 in St Mary's Hall, Calton, Glasgow. It was noted that there were still many within the East End of Glasgow who were impoverished, and the main object of the football club was to raise "funds for the maintenance of the dinner tables of our needy children".

The Great Famine is also celebrated in song by Celtic supporters. The Pete St John-penned ballad *The Fields of Athenry* struck a chord with the Hoops fans back in the late eighties, and it has become a staple part of the Celtic Park repertoire ever since.

The featured jersey was worn by right-back Mikael Lustig during Celtic's 3-1 league win against Dundee United on 11th May 2014. Celtic were presented with the league trophy – their third-in-a-row – after this convincing victory but, surprisingly, manager Neil Lennon resigned 11 days later.

Mikael Lustig on the ball in the jersey which commemorated National Famine Memorial Day in May 2014

AWAY 2014/15

Match worn by Scott Brown

Many of Celtic's kits had celebrated the club's Irish heritage, but the away strip of 2014/15 was released with the exclamation, 'The Power of Scotland'. In the year of Scotland's independence referendum, the country's reigning football champions elected to wear a tartan jersey.

It was not the first time that tartan had been incorporated into the Celtic design – the European kit of five years previous had included tartan shoulder trims and shorts – but this time the entire concept was based around the idea.

The shirt, shorts and socks were all predominantly dark green, with yellow detail included on the round-neck collar and sleeve cuffs, whilst the detail of light green and yellow was an enlarged section of the club's official tartan.

The kit made its first appearance in the Champions League third qualifying round on 30th July 2014, away to Poland's Legia Warsaw, who comprehensively dismantled Ronny Deila's Celtic during a 4-1 victory. The home side also missed two penalties, and defender Efe Ambrose was ordered off in what was a miserable evening of European football for Celtic. On this occasion, Celtic wore Tennent's as their sponsors in place of Magners along with white shorts.

The featured jersey is from Celtic's Europa League campaign, which followed their eventual elimination from the 2014/15 Champions League. The competition crest and UEFA's 'Respect' patches are present on the sleeves of the jersey which was prepared for, and probably worn by, captain Scott Brown for one of two matches. The first was a 2-2 draw with FC Salzburg on the day of Scotland's independence referendum on 18th September 2014, the second was a 1-1 draw with Romanian side FC Astra two months later.

Scott Brown is mobbed by his team-mates after scoring against Austria's FC Salzburg in the Europa League

THIRD 2014/15

Match prepared for Leigh Griffiths

Nike's final kit for Celtic was this third-choice outfit for the 2014/15 campaign. It was cut from the same cloth as their popular 2006-08 European strip, and worked just as well.

The largely all-white affair had yellow and green trim bands across the chest of the jersey, green trim on the sleeves, a green Nike swoosh and a yellow star above a full-colour four-leaf clover crest. The white shorts and socks had minimal green detail, and there was a quote on the inside of the neck, which read, "A club like no other."

This phrase was born from the club's earliest *raison d'etre* – charity. Catalan giants Barcelona have long styled themselves as '*Mes que un club*' – 'More than a club' – and the statement Nike's kit designers incorporated into this particular shirt evoked the similar sentiments that lie at the heart of Celtic. Barcelona's legendary midfielder Xavi once succinctly explained the parallels between the two clubs when he stated that: "Celtic, like Barcelona, are more than a football club. Our clubs are a symbol of a culture and community that has not always been made welcome in their respective countries."

It is certainly a motto that chimed with the supporters and has been echoed by the club's custodians. In 2016, chief executive Peter Lawwell said of the Celtic FC Foundation: "Celtic's origins ensure we are a club like no other and I am proud that today, almost 130 years after the club's formation, we continue to honour our charitable beginnings."

The featured jersey is from the Europa League defeat at the hands of Dinamo Zagreb on 11th December 2014, when striker Leigh Griffiths was an unused substitute.

Leigh Griffiths in action wearing Nike's final Celtic change kit

IN A LEAGUE OF THEIR OWN

Celtic have appeared in 35 Scottish League Cup Finals, winning 20 of them, but bespoke match jerseys have only been worn since 1978*

Following the launch of the Scottish League Cup in 1946, it took Celtic Football Club 11 attempts before they won it for the first time in 1956. However, between the 1964/65 and 1977/78 seasons the club contested an astonishing 14 consecutive finals.

Up until the very last of these, Celtic's League Cup Final jerseys were no different from the ones they wore every other week. However, for the 1978 final against Rangers, the club produced a match-specific shirt complete with red embroidered match details just as they had done for the 1977 Scottish Cup Final at the end of the previous season. From then on the jerseys worn in all of Celtic's subsequent League Cup Final appearances have included the addition of specific match details.

As the selected examples on the following pages show, these have invariably been standard shirts with match detail either embroidered or heat-pressed. However, for the 1982 and 1984 finals, both against Rangers, the same shirt design was worn albeit with subtle but significant differences between the two jerseys. For the 1982 final (which Celtic won 2-1), the club crest and a white Umbro logo appeared on a green hoop, while the match detail was embroidered in black on the white hoops above and below the crest. For the 1984 final (a 3-2 defeat after extra-time), the crest and

green Umbro emblem were positioned on a white hoop, with the match embroidery applied in white on the green hoops above and below the crest (*see page 272*).

Celtic legend Tommy Burns is pictured during the first League Cup Final in 1978 for which the hoops were adorned with bespoke match embroidery (far right)

*Statistics correct up until start of 2022/23 season

SCOTTISH LEAGUE CUP FINAL 1978

Match worn by Roy Aitken

LEAGUE CUP FINAL 1982/83

Celtic 2 Rangers 1, 4th December 1982

LEAGUE CUP FINAL 1983/84

Celtic 2 Rangers 3, 25th March 1984

LEAGUE CUP FINAL 1990/91

Celtic 1 Rangers 2, 28th October 1990

LEAGUE CUP FINAL 2000/01

Celtic 3 Kilmarnock 0, 18th March 2001
Match worn by Johan Mjällby

LEAGUE CUP FINAL 2008/09

Celtic 2 Rangers 0 (aet), 15th March 2009

Match worn by Darren O'Dea

LEAGUE CUP FINAL 2011/12

Celtic 0 Kilmarnock 1, 18th March 2012

Match worn by Anthony Stokes

LEAGUE CUP FINAL 2016/17

Celtic 3 Aberdeen 0, 27th November 2016

Match worn by Scott Brown

LEAGUE CUP FINAL 2017/18

Celtic 2 Motherwell 0, 26th November 2017

Match worn by Olivier Ntcham

CHAPTER EIGHT

NEW KIT ON THE BLOCK

NEW BALANCE 2015-20

HOME 2015/16

Match worn by Leigh Griffiths

Boston-based sports giant New Balance agreed a five-year contract with Celtic in 2015, which was described by the club as a "record-breaking deal". The American company had entered the football shirt market that year by producing kits for the likes of Liverpool, Sevilla and Porto, stating that they wanted "to be on the European stage and also the global stage", adding that, "Celtic fans are everywhere in the world".

Not since the 1993-95 home shirt had Celtic displayed as few as four hoops, so this jersey represented a bold move. Like that Umbro shirt from more than two decades before, the green hoops were once again framed above and below by thin horizontal pinstripes. Like the home tops of 1991-93, 2001-03, 2005-07 and 2008-10, the hoops on the sleeves also extended up, across the shoulders, to the neck. On the inside of the neck an inscription read, "A club like no other", which had become something of an official motto.

Magners continued as the main shirt sponsor for this season. However, for a number of European games (in countries where the advertising of alcohol is banned) their logo was replaced with the emblem of the club's charitable arm, the Celtic FC Foundation.

The featured Celtic Foundation version of the jersey was worn by striker Leigh Griffiths in the scoreless Champions League qualifying round draw with Qarabag in Azerbaijan on 5th August 2015. During the 2015/16 campaign, Griffiths became just the eighth player in Celtic history to score 40 or more goals in a season.

Ronny Deila had visited Celtic Park as a spectator for the first time on the momentous night that his predecessor, Neil Lennon, masterminded an unlikely victory against Xavi's Barcelona in 2012, but the Norwegian was never able to replicate such heights during his own two-year spell in Glasgow. Although Deila won his second title in 2015/16 – Celtic's fifth in succession – European progress was not forthcoming and he stepped down at the end of the campaign.

Above: Leigh Griffiths applauds the travelling Celtic fans after the 0-0 draw against Qarabag in Azerbaijan when the Celtic Foundation version of the jersey was worn

Right: An example of the Magners-sponsored version, complete with 'Premiership Champions 2015/16' detail

AWAY 2015/16

Match worn by Stefan Johansen

New Balance had clearly leafed through the kits of yore when designing their first Celtic away strip. For the away jersey they opted for a revamp of the shirt made famous by Celtic's 1982 victory over Ajax. Many Celtic fans felt that this was long overdue and the jersey became universally popular amongst Hoops supporters.

The kit (featuring the Magners logo) got its first outing against David Moyes' Real Sociedad in a 1-0 pre-season victory on 10th July 2015. The featured jersey is likely to have been worn by Stefan Johansen in Celtic's 4-1 victory over Iceland's Stjarnan in the second qualifying round of the Champions League on 22nd July 2015.

Sleeves patches were not worn in this pre-group stage match and the Celtic FC Foundation logo is featured in place of the sponsor on the front.

THIRD 2015/16

Match worn by Kris Commons

The black hoops of New Balance's iteration of the famous 'Bumblebee' kit were more in keeping with the original than other recent efforts in that they were made up of different widths. However, the top of the jersey had no hoops, just the bright yellow that extended to the shorts and socks (which also featured black hoops). The feature of the crest being presented in one colour is something that New Balance continued to implement on Celtic's change kits.

The promotional video for this shirt was memorable, as the club took us into the famous Celtic huddle on what looked to be a European night under the floodlights. Goalkeeper Craig Gordon, captain Scott Brown, Swedish defender Mikael Lustig and striker Leigh Griffiths all looked on intently during a staged last-minute team talk that ended with the accompanying marketing campaign's 'Live for Celtic' tagline.

HOME 2016/17

Match worn by Scott Brown

An air of revolution filled Kerrydale Street on 23rd May 2016 as 13,000 supporters made their way to Celtic Park to witness the unveiling of Ronny Deila's successor. Newly-installed manager Brendan Rodgers soon had the assembled hordes in raptures by evoking memories of the late, great Tommy Burns, whom Rodgers had previously worked with at Reading.

"Tommy said to me that, 'When you become the Celtic manager, you are a leader of the men and a leader of the people,'" Rodgers told the crowd.

The jersey that was worn during Rodgers' debut season was pitched as being 'Like No Other', and the campaign in which it was worn certainly lived up to that billing.

The five green hoops – which New Balance described as being "fern green and optic white" – included a gradient effect similar to that used on the 2003 UEFA Cup Final jersey, while a gold trim was included along the sleeve cuffs and shoulder seams. This use of gold extended to the star above the full-colour crest, and the Dafabet sponsor's logo was confined to a single green hoop, with Magners – now a secondary sponsor – being consigned to the rear of the jersey. The shorts and socks were again predominantly white, with gold piping on the shorts and a thick green band around the stockings.

Rodgers' inaugural speech was the ideal introduction to what would be the perfect maiden season – an 'invincible' campaign which saw the club winning its first domestic treble in 16 years. It was only the fourth time that Celtic had accomplished this feat, with Rodgers joining the names of Jock Stein (who won it in 1967 and 1969) and Martin O'Neill (2001) in that illustrious managerial honours list.

The jersey featured on these pages was worn by captain Scott Brown in one of the five European matches in which Celtic wore the Dafabet logo on the front of the home jersey, with the Celtic FC Foundation logo to the rear in place of the Magners logo when local advertising laws required.

Above: Scott Brown marshals the troops against Borussia Mönchengladbach

Left: The Celtic FC Foundation logo appeared on the back of this jersey in five European matches

AWAY 2016/17

Match worn by Scott Brown

New Balance's 2016/17 home and away strips were unveiled with the marketing slogan 'Like No Other' and the black and gold away jersey again featured the words 'A club like no other' on the internal hem.

The featured jersey was worn by Scott Brown in the end-of-season Celtic FC Foundation charity match on 28th May 2017. This was the day after Brendan Rodgers' side had become 'invincible' treble-winners, and the match also signalled the end of Kris Commons' Parkhead career.

The game was contested between two teams comprised of ex-players and Celtic-supporting celebrities – one captained by Henrik Larsson (Henrik's Heroes) and one by Lubo Moravčík (Lubo's Legends). Larsson's side won 5-2 in front of a capacity Celtic Park crowd.

THIRD 2016/17

Match worn by Kieran Tierney

The fitting advertising tagline that accompanied Celtic's 2016/17 kits was, 'If You Know Your History'. As the club celebrated the 50th anniversary of becoming the first British team to win the European Cup, it launched an alternative kit that saw manufacturers New Balance throw caution to the wind.

Taking inspiration from history – specifically the pink and brown ticket for the 1967 European Cup Final – New Balance pitched both brown and pink away strip concepts to a focus group of supporters. The group gave the pink jersey the green light and this eye-catching creation was born.

Despite strictly being a 2016/17 kit, the shirt pictured here was worn the following season by left-back Kieran Tierney at Easter Road against Hibernian on either 7th December 2017 or 21st April 2018.

SCOTTISH CUP FINAL 2017

Match prepared for Moussa Dembélé

Some time after winning the 2017 Scottish Cup Final, Brendan Rodgers revealed to the *Celtic View* what he had said to his players before the game. "We'd celebrated going unbeaten in the league, and then we celebrated the Lisbon Lions," he explained. "At Hampden it was up to us. No one was going to write about it if we didn't do it. We had to go out and do it."

Rodgers' winning mentality was never more evident than in that breathtaking final match of the 2016/17 season against Aberdeen Celtic's 37th Scottish Cup win was packed with drama from the start: Stuart Armstrong's equaliser a couple of minutes after future Celt Jonny Hayes had given the Dons a ninth-minute lead; a gut-wrenching jaw-break suffered by Kieran Tierney after 26 minutes; Tierney's replacement, Tom Rogic, picking the ball up after 92 minutes, magically weaving through the Aberdeen defence and slotting his shot low under Joe Lewis to decide the match.

One player not immediately associated with this era-defining victory is Moussa Dembélé. The Frenchman was just 20 years of age when Rodgers made him his first Celtic signing in June 2016. Such was the prolific striker's impact, the £500,000 paid to Fulham was recouped 40-fold when he departed two years later to join Lyon.

The jersey featured here was worn by Dembélé as he returned to the Celtic bench at Hampden, having recovered from an injury sustained in the semi-final the previous month. Although he was an unused substitute in the final, arguably no other player had contributed more to getting Celtic to Scottish football's showpiece fixture, scoring five goals in the first three rounds against Albion Rovers (3-0), Inverness (6-0) and St Mirren (4-1).

Sadly, Dembélé's hamstring had given way during Celtic's 2-0 semi-final victory over Rangers, and he narrowly lost his battle to be fit for the final in which Celtic wrapped up their fourth-ever domestic treble. However, the 32 goals that he contributed throughout the 2016/17 season wearing this classy set of New Balance hoops went a long way to crystallising Celtic's veneer of invincibility.

The Celtic players, including unused sub Moussa Dembélé (right), celebrate securing the quadruple with victory in the 2017 Scottish Cup Final

HOME 2017/18

Match worn by Scott Brown

There are four bronze statues outside Celtic Park to commemorate some of the most celebrated figures from the club's history. The fact that three of these – Jock Stein, Billy McNeill and Jimmy Johnstone – were part of Celtic's European Cup triumph in 1967 illustrates the magnitude of that side's achievements.

Two days after the 50th anniversary of that famous victory, Celtic paid tribute to their greatest side by clinching an 'invincible' treble against Aberdeen in the 2017 Scottish Cup Final. For the following season, kit manufacturers New Balance paid a further salute to the Lions by designing a modern classic of a jersey.

The marketing campaign for the 2017/18 home shirt implored the club's supporters to 'Live the Legend' and the kit that it referred to was a fine tribute to the legendary Lisbon side.

The crest, New Balance logo, as well as the front and rear sponsors, player names and numbers were all printed on the jersey in gold, along with text around the badge which commemorated the anniversary with the words, "*Lisboa. 50° Aniversario. 25 de Maio de 1967.*" Perhaps the only negative in the design was the fact that, in a change to the previous season's jersey, the Dafabet logo was spread over two hoops (and in fact overlapped two more).

There was an inevitable feeling among Celtic supporters that the achievements of Brendan Rodgers' 2016/17 side could not be emulated in the Northern Irishman's second season, such was the otherworldly nature of his first campaign. His maiden season had seen a domestic whitewash with no other Scottish team able to lay a glove on his unbeatable side.

However, although the previous season's league-winning margin was cut from 30 to nine points in 2017/18 by Aberdeen (with Celtic succumbing to four league defeats across the campaign), remarkably Rodgers became the first manager in the history of Scottish football to win back-to-back trebles – the 'Double Treble'.

Above: The 2017/18 home jersey smartly commemorated the 50th anniversary of the Lisbon Lions

Right: The use of gold on the crest was a stylish touch

AWAY 2017/18

Match worn by Leigh Griffiths

This jersey was part of Celtic's 50th anniversary collection to commemorate the Lisbon Lions' European Cup victory. Back in 1967, Celtic's away colours were all-green, and this updated version of that design – and its advertising slogan exhorting fans to 'Live the Legend' – was a hit with supporters.

The jersey's crest featured Lisbon 50th anniversary detail, and inside the back of the neck a small detail of green and white hoops was set beside the black and blue stripes of Inter Milan.

The featured jersey was worn on 2nd August 2017 against Rosenberg in the Champions League qualifier in Norway and is unique in that it has no sponsor on the front, but has the Celtic FC Foundation crest on the back.

THIRD 2017/18

Match worn by Moussa Dembélé

Another nod to the past was evident in the third kit for the 2017/18 campaign. Reminiscent of Nike's change outfit of 2010/11, the tone used by New Balance for this jersey was described as 'cactus green'.

As part of the Lisbon Lions' 50th anniversary celebrations, the crest included the commemorative lettering and the inside of the neck also featured the Celtic hoops and Inter Milan stripes motif. The sleeves of this jersey have faint hoops within the material – a subtle detail in keeping with the overall simplicity of the kit.

The match worn jersey featured here was issued to French striker Moussa Dembélé who lined up against Neil Lennon's Hibernian at Hampden Park for the League Cup semi-final on 21st October 2017. Celtic replaced their black shorts with cactus green alternatives for the occasion.

HOME 2018/19

Match worn by Kristoffer Ajer

The promotional campaign for all three Celtic kits for the 2018/19 season carried the marketing slogan, 'Only the Bold'.

This may well have derived from the roots of the club's official nickname, 'The Bhoys', which can be traced back to a promotional postcard from the early 20th century (featuring a moustachioed Celt wearing the club's kit and standing below an Irish harp with four shamrocks underneath) which referenced Celtic as 'The Bould Bhoys'. Celtic's Irish roots meant that in their early years they were often referred to as 'The Bhoys', from the Irish pronunciation of the word 'Boy'.

For their fourth Celtic home jersey, New Balance took inspiration from Celtic's first-ever set of hoops from some 115 years earlier, with the round, buttoned collar evoking the club's original set of hooped jerseys. The white panels under the arms, however, appeared to conflict with this admirable historic approach and is a design element which has been greeted with some consternation by traditionalist supporters when it had been employed in the past.

The jersey incorporated a subtle, tartan-effect pattern, and the club crest returned to the full-colour, embroidered version with the star in gold above. The Dafabet logo was once again placed over several hoops and was far more prominent than on the previous season's jersey thanks to its black and yellow colour scheme. The shorts were again white, and the socks returned to full green and white hoops.

This kit made its first appearance in the last fixture of the 2017/18 season, when Celtic drew 2-2 with a Republic of Ireland Select XI in Scott Brown's testimonial match. The Celtic goals on that day came from Leigh Griffiths and departing Manchester City loanee Patrick Roberts, who had endeared himself to Celtic fans over the previous two and a half seasons at Parkhead.

Norwegian defender Kristoffer Ajer in the jersey inspired by Celtic's first-ever set of hoops

AWAY 2018/19

Match prepared for James Forrest

White away jerseys seem to strike a chord with Celtic supporters, and on this popular shirt the commemorative celtic cross crest that was designed to celebrate the club's 125th anniversary in 2012 made a welcome reappearance.

The shirt was unveiled (without player names) for a pre-season friendly against Shamrock Rovers, but it wasn't worn again until a 6-0 league victory away to St Johnstone three months later. The wearer of the featured jersey, James Forrest, ran riot in the Perth rain that day and scored an emphatic four first-half goals.

Worn far less frequently than the black and yellow third outfit, Celtic only wore this away jersey on one further occasion (against Hamilton on 24th November 2018) in the run-in to their third consecutive domestic treble. This makes obtaining a player version extremely challenging for collectors.

THIRD 2018/19

Match prepared for Oliver Burke

Celtic's away jerseys had been fairly simple in their style until the radical Umbro designs of the 1980s and 1990s. Nike also had their quirkier moments some years later with the black-and-yellow-quartered effort (2011/12), and with their use of tartan (2009/10 and 2014/15). It was no surprise, then, when New Balance went bold with Celtic's striking third kit in 2018/19.

The jersey made regular appearances during a lengthy European campaign – against Rosenborg (when it was worn with yellow shorts rather than the usual black), FK Suduva, RB Leipzig and Valencia – which saw them fall at the third hurdle in Champions League qualifying before reaching the last 32 of the Europa League.

The shirt pictured here was prepared for European competition, with Europa League and UEFA 'Respect' sleeve patches and the European names and numbers set.

HOME 2019/20

Match worn by Scott Sinclair

The fifth and final Celtic home kit from New Balance was launched for the club's historic tilt at 'nine-in-a-row,' as well as a monumental quadruple-treble. Both of these seemingly unthinkable accolades were achieved, despite the football calendar being curtailed early in March 2020 due to the Covid-19 pandemic.

'On To Victory' was the advertising tagline adopted by New Balance when the promotional video for the new strip dropped on the club's official channel on 1st May 2019. As well as club captain Scott Brown and stalwarts Nir Bitton and Callum McGregor, the marketing campaign also featured homegrown hero Kieran Tierney. Tierney, however, would never kick a ball wearing this kit as, much to the chagrin of his adoring army of Celtic fans, he left for Arsenal in a £25 million transfer in August 2019.

The jersey itself featured a classic green button-down collar, with a white section extending across the shoulders and down the sleeves of the shirt at the expense of green hoops which gave the overall design a polo-shirt appeal.

The first of five green hoops ran below the bottom collar button, and the prominent Dafabet logo dominated three of these in the centre of the shirt, with Magners once again appearing on the back of the jersey above the players' names. A small celtic cross detail appeared on the back of the neck, below the collar. The manufacturer's 'NB' logo appeared in black, as did flashes on each sleeve. The kit was finished off with white shorts and green and white socks.

The featured jersey was worn by Scott Sinclair – who had been a fans' favourite under Brendan Rodgers since signing from Aston Villa in 2016 – against Motherwell in a 5-2 win on 10th August 2019.

Scott Sinclair cuts in from the touchline wearing the final New Balance Celtic home jersey

AWAY 2019/20

Match worn by Scott Sinclair

The final away jersey of the New Balance era got off to a less than auspicious start during the pre-season of 2019/20. The yellow and green strip was scheduled to be worn during Celtic's tour of Austria and Switzerland, but the jerseys weren't packed with the rest of the kit so when the team took to the field against St Gallen they were wearing the new away shorts and socks but with a green training top with hastily applied white numbers on the back.

When they were finally worn, the 'missing' jerseys were warmly received. The round-neck, button collar harked back to the home jersey of the previous season, and there was a subtle tartan pattern running through the green on the shoulders and arms.

The featured jersey was worn by Scott Sinclair in the 1–1 draw against Hibernian on 28th September 2019.

THIRD 2019/20

Unworn player shirt

Umbro's fan-designed white, black and green 1986/87 third jersey may never have been worn in a competitive match, but it went on to become something of a cult favourite. The next release that was never given an airing by the club came 33 years later, but New Balance's grey and pink effort is unlikely ever to be included in any list of classic Celtic kits.

The club claimed that the pink chevron was inspired by the change kit of 1919/20, but the response from Celtic supporters on fan forums and social media was largely negative, with comments ranging from "horrific" to "a monstrosity". It remains to be seen if this jersey will build a fanbase over time, but Umbro's zigzag effort of 1991/92 proved that anything is possible.

The featured player-issue jersey was provided by Celtic Football Club, but as it was never match prepared there are no sleeve patches, player name or squad number.

PARADISE LOST

From the 1930s onwards there are just three Celtic jerseys that are 'missing in action' from the collection within the pages of this book

Celtic line up against Kilmarnock in March 1965 in green shirts with white collar and cuffs – one of the very few match worn jerseys missing from this book

Sadly, there are no known surviving jerseys from the early history of Celtic FC. Not only would these kits have been worn until they fell apart, there was simply no concept around the club of their potential future value – in both historic and financial terms.

Even up until relatively recently, the Celtic kitman was driven primarily by economic considerations and sets of hoops were far more likely to have ended up as rags for cleaning the dressing room than framed in the Club Museum.

Fortunately, thanks in no small part to kitman Neilly Mochan's incredible collection as well as a small band of dedicated Celtic shirt collectors, we have been able to assemble this unique and historic set of jerseys, which includes a match worn or match prepared example of almost every jersey – home and away – worn by the club from the 1930s onwards.

In fact, from the post-war period, in the course of the five years in which *The Celtic Jersey* has been in production, the author has tracked down every single jersey bar three change jerseys from the 1960s and '70s. Perhaps someone, somewhere will have them in their collection, but until they are discovered here are the ones that got away...

"The author has tracked down every single jersey bar three change jerseys from the 1960s and '70s"

THIRD 1964/65 & AWAY 1965/66

In the two games directly prior to Jock Stein's first match in charge of Celtic on 10th March 1965, the club played Kilmarnock at home – once in the league and once in the Scottish Cup.

It was not unknown at this time for Celtic to wear their away kit at home for matches against teams like Kilmarnock – whose blue and white stripes were close to Celtic's home colours – if the away side arrived with their home kit. So, in the league encounter Celtic wore a green away jersey with white collar and cuffs; in the Scottish Cup, they wore the 'Shamrock' jersey. The latter was never worn during Stein's tenure, but the green kit with white collar and cuffs – usually worn with green shorts and white socks – continued to get an airing until it was replaced with the all-green alternative in 1966.

This jersey was a generic 'off the peg' Umbro design without a club crest, and even if a shirt of this style were discovered today it would be difficult to authenticate it as a match worn Celtic shirt unless it came directly from a player. It is most likely that after the first team had finished wearing them that these jerseys would have become training kit and ultimately ended up being cut up for cleaning rags.

Above: Midfielder Bobby Murdoch is pictured in the rarely used supporter-designed 1973-76 away strip

AWAY 1973-76

One Monday morning in 1973, Celtic photographer Hugh Birt received a call from Jock Stein. Birt was asked to head directly to Celtic Park as the club had taken delivery of a brand-new away kit from Umbro and Stein wanted it photographed. Hugh duly obliged and was supplied with Bobby Murdoch as his model for the morning.

The black-and-green-striped jersey had been designed by supporter Gordon Cowan as part of a 'Pick-a-Strip' competition in the *Celtic View*. Cowan's design had been selected by Jock Stein and the Celtic board as the winner, and their choice was announced on 12th September 1973.

As with all away designs at the time, the kit was rarely used although it did see action from time to time, notably against Preston North End (featuring Bobby Charlton) in a 2-1 friendly defeat on 2nd August 1974.

AWAY 1975-77

During the mid-1970s Celtic wore a canary yellow and green away kit. The jerseys featured the v-insert collar that was fashionable at the time and was found on the home kit. The style was memorably worn against Boavista in the European Cup Winners' Cup second round first leg in Portugal on 22nd October 1975. The match ended goalless, and Celtic were able to progress with a 3-1 victory at home a fortnight later.

Like the other missing jerseys from this collection, without a club crest it would be extremely difficult to authenticate any example that surfaced as a match worn Celtic jersey. However, as it was used in Europe it is quite possible that some players swapped with their opponents and maybe there is one out there somewhere in the collection of a Portuguese player or even in the stadium vaults at Boavista.

"The black-and green-striped jersey had been designed by supporter Gordon Cowan as part of a 'Pick-a-Strip' competition in the Celtic View"

Below: Celtic take on Boavista of Portugal in the rarely worn yellow and green kit in 1975

OTHER RARE JERSEYS

In addition to the handful of shirts missing from *The Celtic Jersey* collection, there are also some rare and unusual kits that, whilst still highly desirable to collectors, cannot be classed as 'official' tops.

One of these is a green jersey with narrow white stripes that was worn in a practice game in the late 1960s. There are black and white photographs of the team wearing these jerseys and a colour photograph of Jock Stein wearing the style during the same period while the Celtic squad were training at Seamill Hydro on the Ayrshire coast. It is possible that this was a set of jerseys that was considered as an away style, or they could have been purchased purely as training kit. What is absolutely certain is that they were never worn in a competitive match.

During a pre-season tour of Australia in 1977, Celtic lined up for six friendly matches wearing their distinctive green and white hoops in short sleeves with a v-neck and no club crest. These were only worn on this tour, with the jersey of the previous season – which had the white floppy collar and v-insert – being used again for the following campaign in 1977/78. The pre-season tour shirt was different for some reason and resembled a later 1980s design.

Left: The shirts worn for the pre-season tour to Australia in the summer of 1977 had no club crest and a different collar to the jersey worn once the domestic season began

Celtic defeated Red Star Belgrade in their final game of the tour and were pictured lifting the trophy wearing their opponents' shirts, having swapped jerseys after the final whistle. It is not beyond the realms of possibility, therefore, that Neilly Mochan, the kitman at the time, deliberately used an alternative set of shirts throughout this tour to ensure he had enough match jerseys for the start of the new season.

Additionally, as Celtic moved into their 10th season without a league title in 1997/98, their shirt sponsorship deal with CR Smith was about to expire. The new home jersey was photographed for the weekly *Shoot!* magazine with the old sponsor across the front, however by the time the season kicked off the actual match jerseys carried the name and logo of kit manufacturer Umbro. At least one 1997/98 CR Smith jersey made its way into the hands of a collector, but the jersey in this incarnation was never worn during a match.

Below: Jock Stein is pictured in the mysterious green with thin white stripes jersey which was worn during Celtic training sessions in the 1960s (below right)

Below: A rare 'CR Smith' prototype version of the 1997/98 hoops. By the time the season started the sponsor had changed to Umbro

CHAPTER NINE

HOOPS, STARS AND STRIPES

ADIDAS 2020-

HOME 2020/21

Match worn by Odsonne Édouard

On 13th March 2020, Celtic announced the most lucrative kit deal in Scottish sporting history when they signed a five-year partnership with German sportswear goliaths adidas.

This tie-in arrived just in time for a season that had been a decade in the making; one that a whole generation had waited their entire lives for – Celtic were going for their tenth league title in-a-row.

The advertising campaign for the new kit naturally homed in on the ten-in-a-row furore, with the slogan, "Not for second best. Nine and counting. One decade in the making. Here we go", and the debut kit from adidas was fit for a team which had utterly dominated Scottish football in recent years with four back-to-back trebles.

Not only did adidas apply their legendary three stripes to the shoulders of the Celtic jersey, they also provided a generous helping of seven complete green hoops to the body of their first home shirt. The green round-neck collar featured a yellow trim, which had last been seen on the Celtic home shirt of 2008-10. As well as being used on the sleeve trims, the star above the crest, and on the Dafabet logo, yellow was also present on a four-leaf clover detail to the rear of the jersey, just under the collar. The famous adidas stripes ran down the white shorts and along the tops of the socks to complete what was a classic-looking Celtic outfit.

The season of Celtic fans' dreams, however, turned into a nightmare as Neil Lennon's side capitulated in empty stadiums, with supporters still not permitted to attend matches due to the Covid-19 pandemic. The manager was relieved of his duties on 24th February 2021 as the Hoops spiralled towards their first trophyless campaign in 11 years.

The jersey featured here was worn by Odsonne Édouard, who claimed the accolade of 'top goalscorer' in an otherwise forgettable season.

Odsonne Édouard in action against Rangers in Celtic's first adidas kit

AWAY 2020/21

Match worn by Kristoffer Ajer

Celtic's first adidas away shirt recreated the kit worn when the club famously won the league at Love Street on the final day of the 1985/86 season. There had been earlier attempts at rebooting this popular strip (by Nike in 2010/11 and New Balance in 2017/18), but adidas got the remake pretty much spot on.

Previous efforts at recreating the spirit of Love Street had failed by using black accents and shorts, but adidas used two tones of green to brilliant effect.

This kit made its competitive debut against Kilmarnock on 9th August 2020, when Celtic dropped points in just their second league match of the season.

The featured shirt was worn by Norwegian defender Kris Ajer, whose performances earned him a £14 million move to Brentford at the end of the season.

THIRD 2020/21

Match worn by Scott Brown

Manufacturers adidas claimed that their stylish first Celtic third kit was, "Not for the ordinary". It was, their marketing campaign explained, "For the disco lights. For the paradise nights. And the glow of glory."

The black third jersey was based on the adidas 'Condivo' template and the club crest was adapted with the four-leaf clover embroidered without a circular border.

Undoubtedly adidas came close to producing the finest set of Celtic jerseys in the modern era in 2020/21, but the memory of them is certainly tarnished by the team's poor performances on the park.

The featured jersey was worn by captain Scott Brown who, prior to leaving Celtic at the end of this campaign, became one of just seven players to have appeared 600 or more times for the club.

HOME 2021/22

Match worn by Kyogo Furuhashi

The arrival of adidas – only Celtic's fourth kit suppliers in 132 years – and their legendary three stripes had been welcomed by those Celtic fans with a passion for football jerseys, and their first set of kits certainly did not disappoint. The football team on the park, however, fell somewhere short of what the Celtic support had come to expect over the previous decade, and huge changes were required for the 2021/22 campaign.

The club announced the arrival of the 2021/22 home jersey by declaring that with "unbroken hoops" came an "unbroken history", in a thinly veiled swipe at their Glasgow rivals, Rangers, who had halted Celtic's march to 'ten-in-a-row' the previous season.

Clearly Celtic were up for the battle to regain their league title and, whilst wholesale changes were beginning to materialise within the football department following the arrival of new manager Ange Postecoglou, adidas gave the new home kit a more nuanced update.

The round-neck on the new jersey was plain white and each of the seven green hoops had horizontal pinstripes above and below them, similar to those added by Umbro in the mid-1980s and by New Balance in 2015/16. The Dafabet sponsor's logo reverted from black to white, but the adidas logos on the jersey, shorts and socks appeared in black. It was a simple but effective design, which fared Celtic well as they went on to win the league and League Cup double in Postecoglou's first season in charge.

The Australian manager had arrived from Japanese side Yokohama F. Marinos, and he brought four Japanese players to Scotland as he rebuilt a Celtic side lacking confidence and flair. One of those players, Kyogo Furuhashi – who wore the jersey featured here – swiftly became a hero of Celtic supporters all over the world.

Kyogo Furuhashi did the Celtic jersey proud during his first season at Parkhead

AWAY 2021/22

Match prepared for Dane Murray

Gold had appeared on Celtic away kits a few times previously, but adidas approached its addition somewhat differently, matching it with dark green for a kit that they proclaimed was for, "Real fans… Real football… Since 1888."

The colourway worked brilliantly, with the three adidas stripes returning to the shoulders. Like the black third kit of the previous season, the circular borders were absent from the crest and the four-leaf clover was enlarged.

This kit is perhaps most fondly remembered for being worn in the League Cup Final win over Hibernian which earned Ange Postecoglou his first Scottish silverware.

The featured jersey was prepared for Dane Murray, who was an unused substitute for the Europa League match away to Ferencváros on 4th November 2021, when the usual Dafabet branding was replaced with the Celtic FC Foundation logo.

THIRD 2021/22

Match prepared for Georgios Giakoumakis

Until Celtic Park received a facelift for the centenary season of 1987/88, its main entrance was an imposing metal double-door, painted and repainted green over the years. Above this unremarkable entrance to 95 Kerrydale Street was a stunning stained glass window with a floral pattern and the words 'Celtic FC' amongst a flurry of greens and pinks. The glass was thought to have been destroyed during the installation of the new fascia, but it was later discovered behind the new entrance wall and restored. It is now on display within the corridors of Paradise.

It was the beauty of this stained glass that inspired Celtic's 2021/22 third kit, with the floral pattern appearing on the inner neck, and the green and pink of the glass used in alternating pinstripes on the white body.

The featured jersey was Europa League-prepared for, but not worn by, Georgios Giakoumakis.

HOME 2022/23

Match worn by Callum McGregor

Kit manufacturer adidas thickened the hoops for their third incarnation of the Celtic hoops, with the 2022/23 edition comprising of four complete green hoops, with two additional incomplete hoops visible at the top and bottom of the jersey.

Rather than green, which had been used in the two previous home designs, the three adidas stripes on the shoulders were applied in a metallic silver material, which was replicated on the shorts and socks.

Silver was also chosen to create the European Cup star, which had been embroidered in gold on the previous six jerseys, above the club crest. This was the first time the star had appeared in silver on the home jersey, but it matched the colour of the European trophy it represented so it felt appropriate.

The round-neck used previously by adidas was replaced with a classy v-neck, and the green hoops included a subtle, shaded pattern throughout. The socks returned to green and white hoops for the first time since 2018/19.

The marketing campaign for this jersey included the words to the popular Celtic chant, "We're on our way to Paradise", and there was a genuine belief amongst supporters that, unlike some previous seasons, all the star players who featured in the pre-season promotional shoot would remain at the club to build on the foundations laid by Ange Postecoglou the previous season.

The featured jersey was prepared for club stalwart Callum McGregor who took over the captaincy from Scott Brown at the beginning of Postecoglou's reign. At 29, McGregor led Celtic into the 2022/23 season on the back of a league and League Cup double, with his legendary status already assured, by virtue of his contribution to four back-to-back domestic trebles.

Callum McGregor in action against Real Madrid at Celtic Park in September 2022

AWAY 2022/23

Match prepared for Jota

Manufacturer adidas pulled off a masterstroke in their debut season with Celtic by recreating the spirit of Love Street '86 for the club's away strip, and their reimagining of the iconic lime green kit was hugely popular. For their third season, the kit designers decided to delve back into the back catalogue in search of another classic.

The early nineties were not kind to the Parkhead side, but the black Umbro away kit with green and white stripes that was worn from 1992-94 was one of the finest of any era. The adidas reboot some 30 years later became an instant hit, with initial sales making it the most popular Celtic change kit of modern times.

The featured jersey was prepared for Portuguese winger Jota, whose name appears below a subtle 'Celtic FC' detail, once again inspired by the stained glass that once sat above the entrance to Parkhead.

THIRD 2022/23

Match worn by Kyogo Furuhashi

The last time a Celtic jersey dared to use grey as the main colour was back in 2019/20 when New Balance released the grey and pink jersey that was never worn. It was, therefore, a bold move by adidas to retrace a path that had previously proven unsuccessful.

This time, the jersey colourway was more subtle, with bright yellow being used on the club's crest and star, adidas and sponsor logos as well as the three shoulder stripes. The black sleeve cuffs included an interesting detail, inspired by the geometric outline of Celtic Park as it appears on the Glasgow skyline.

The featured jersey was prepared for Japanese striker Kyogo Furuhashi for Celtic's league encounter against St Mirren on 18th September 2022. This away day ended in disappointment for Ange Postecoglou's men, who succumbed to their first league defeat in nearly a year as the Buddies inflicted a 2-0 reverse to end the champions' 38-match unbeaten streak.

THE CELTIC JERSEY CRAZE

This book would not have been possible without the passion and generosity of the shirt collectors who have taken it upon themselves to gather, safeguard and cherish these snapshots of Celtic's illustrious history

By Paul John Dykes

It was during the writing of my second book – *Celtic's Smiler: The Neilly Mochan Story* – in 2014 that I got to know the late Mochan's son, Neilly Mochan Junior. As part of my research into his father's incredible journey as Celtic player, trainer and kitman, Mochan Junior handed me the keys to a unique family vault. Contained within was 50 years' worth of medals, boots, photographs, tracksuits, kitbags, and match worn jerseys that his father had amassed during a lifetime in football.

Celtic Football Club itself does not possess a vast quantity of historic jerseys, so in order to complete the Celtic match worn jersey chronicles – as Mochan passed away in 1994 – I made contact with an inner sanctum of independent collectors, who all offered their jerseys willingly.

Stuart from *The Celtic Shirt* website was too humble to be interviewed for this feature. He was content with the fact that the book was being compiled so that other match worn shirt enthusiasts could enjoy the site's unique collection. He offered support and advice from day one of this project and many of his jerseys are displayed within this book. I would recommend that you check out his excellent website at **www.thecelticshirt.co.uk**

The following individuals also trusted me with their collections and made this book possible. To a man, they reminded me of a quote from Celtic's first-ever manager, Willie Maley: "My love for Celtic has been a craze."

NEILLY MOCHAN JUNIOR

"Celtic wear all-white with seven green hoops. That is how I see the kit, and the greatest version of it is the one we wore in Lisbon.

"The only reason my dad kept all those old Celtic jerseys was for me. He'd pull a jersey out of his bag when he returned home from a game and throw it over to me. He did have a cupboard at Celtic Park that was rammed full of various items of kit, but he didn't keep the jerseys catalogued at the stadium or anything. This cupboard was famous among the players because no one was allowed access to it. It was situated within the changing room and there was a whole lot of Celtic history in there. I'm willing to guess that he would have had at least one of every Celtic jersey in that cupboard from his time at the club. Not because he was a collector, but because he wouldn't throw them out.

"There were more jerseys in my collection, but some of them have been lost or given away over the years. People from Celtic supporters clubs would come to the house and ask him for a jersey for their annual dance or charity fundraiser, and my dad would duly oblige. I definitely had two Dukla Prague tops from our European Cup semi-final in 1967. I didn't realise their significance at the time, but I remember them standing out because of their unusual colours. I'm not sure where those two jerseys went but they are no longer in my collection.

"There are so many opposition kits in my collection due to the tradition of kitmen swapping jerseys on European nights – my dad was the kitman for every European encounter that Celtic were involved in from 1964 until 1994. Again, it can be difficult to identify the teams and the players who wore them. I was able to confirm that the Ajax top from 1982 was worn by a young Marco van Basten and that the Man Utd jersey used in Lou Macari's testimonial was worn by Lou himself in the first half of the match.

"Some of my jerseys are on display in the National Football Museum in Manchester and the Scottish Football Museum in Glasgow. With the rise of social media and online auction sites, adding to my collection has become easier than ever before and I have no intention of stopping."
Twitter @TheDonsPool

PAUL LAMB

"My earliest memories of Celtic shirts are from the mid-1980s. Danny McGrain is the first player that comes to mind wearing the hoops. I was nine years old in 1984 and Brian McClair was my hero at the time, so those mid-eighties hoops with the large crest on them – before and after the sponsors first appeared – are my most vivid memories.

"The first replica Celtic jersey I remember having was the 1987/88 centenary shirt, and I still have it. I got it for my 13th birthday, which landed in between the league-winning game against Dundee (23rd April 1988) and the Scottish Cup Final against Dundee United (14th May 1988). I can still clearly remember that scorching summer's day, wearing my new hoops with pride while walking up to Hampden with my dad, brother, aunt, uncle and cousins.

"There has been talk of a museum at Celtic Park for years. If this ever happens, I'd happily speak to the club with a view to having some of my collection on display."

MALCOLM McDOUGALL

"I am not a Celtic supporter, so I suppose I am a little different to the rest of the collectors in this book.

"My collection started with replica jerseys of my two teams – Aberdeen and Liverpool – and I then started to pick up shirts in charity shops. I began to add Scotland tops and then any team's jerseys to my collection, which now includes 300 replicas and 75 match worn shirts.

"Jerseys from the 1970s and 1980s are what attract me, and some of my favourites include a white Liverpool away jersey that was worn by Kenny Dalglish and Eric Black's Aberdeen shirt from the 1983 European Cup Winners' Cup Final. I also have a Portugal shirt from the 1966 World Cup finals, and Scotland tops worn by Danny McGrain, Archie Gemmill and Alex McLeish.

"No football jersey collection would be complete without some iconic Celtic shirts, and I have eight match worn Celtic tops, as well as George Connelly's Scottish Cup Final tracksuit top from 1973. The 1986 lime green away jersey and the 1988 centenary shirt are particular favourites from that era. Umbro produced some great jerseys throughout that period and their designs remind me of some great flair teams from the 1970s and 1980s.

"Back in 2010, I came across a Facebook page dedicated to match worn Celtic shirts, and I instantly loved it. I had always been into football tops, which led to me buying all the replica Celtic jerseys and ones from lots of the big European teams, but I never believed I would ever own a player's one. There was a particular post on this page about a Scott McDonald player shirt that was for sale, so I decided to ask for more details about it and became fascinated by the differences between player-specification jerseys and those replica tops I had been buying for years. I decided to buy that McDonald jersey as a gift for my mum, and it still hangs, framed, in my parents' hall.

"About a year later, I saw that the Celtic Charity Fund (now the Celtic FC Foundation) were auctioning some shirts from a testimonial game against Norwich to raise money for the Teenage Cancer Trust as well as themselves. I was lucky enough to get one of

the shirts. The rest, as they say, is history.

"Over the first couple of years my collection grew slowly as I bought jerseys from as far afield as Thailand and Australia. At present, I have about 110 match worn or player-issue shirts, and I still have around 40 replica shirts that I have kept dating from the 1988 centenary season right up to the 2018/19 season.

"The part of my collection I'm most proud of is the testimonial shirts. Back in the day, it seemed that only truly special players stayed at a club long enough to receive a testimonial in recognition of their service. For Danny McGrain's tribute in 1980, the players' shirts had embroidered details around the club badge for the first time in a testimonial. Almost 40 years later, only a further 10 Celtic players have gone on to receive testimonials and I am fortunate enough to have a shirt from every one of those games.

"Most collectors will say that a shirt from the 1967 European Cup Final would be their 'Holy Grail'. If one of those ever becomes available, I know it will have a price tag that is way out of my financial reach, and as such I'm content in the knowledge that I will never own one. There are also some away jerseys that have been worn sparingly over the years, which make them difficult to come by. The one that I'd love to find is the yellow third jersey that was worn in 1984/85 against Rapid Vienna in the away leg of a European Cup Winners' Cup tie."

www.mycelticshirts.co.uk

JOE ARCARI

"Although my dad took me to Celtic games as a toddler – which would have been at the tail end of the nine-in-a-row era – I don't really remember them. I do, however, vividly recall watching Celtic when they wore the 1978/79 home and away jerseys and I am lucky to now own a player's version of both. The three players that I specifically remember from that period are Roy Aitken, Davie Provan and Johnny Doyle. I used to get the three of them mixed up when they were playing because of their curly (probably permed!) hair. I was too young to understand their different positions and we were too far away on the terracing to see the players clearly. Provan became more distinctive once he started wearing his shirt outside his shorts and his socks at his ankles.

"The first Celtic replica jersey I owned was the 1978/79 home kit, which I received on Christmas morning in 1978 along with the magnificent tracksuit from that season.

That campaign ended in high drama as 'Ten Men Won the League' on the last day of the season by beating Rangers 4-2 after Johnny Doyle was sent off.

"I got into collecting match worn jerseys by accident, really. I had replicas of pretty much every Celtic shirt since about 1980 and I started to frame them around 2007 to create a 'Celtic room' within my house (it was meant to be a play room for my two daughters!). Then, in 2012, I noticed that St Mirren's David van Zanten was raising money for Yorkhill Children's Hospital. He lived locally, so I contacted him prior to Celtic playing in Paisley and asked if he could obtain a Celtic jersey for me in return for me making a reasonable donation to the hospital. David arrived at my door a couple of weeks later with Tony Watt's Celtic jersey from the 5-0 win. It was brilliant of David to do this for me, and Yorkhill Hospital also benefitted from the arrangement. After that, I was desperate for more and I've been fortunate to pick up some more top-class jerseys along the way.

"The Jimmy Johnstone jersey that I have is my favourite. I have his number seven shorts as well. I go into my Celtic room, look at Jinky's strip on its mannequin inside its big glass cabinet and admire it for a couple of minutes every day. The big green number sevens stitched on to both sides of the shorts are just magnificent. I miss Celtic having the large green numbers on their shorts, and dearly wish the club would bring them back. They were unique. I love looking at old photographs and seeing those big

green numbers on either side of the shorts. Along with the hoops and the plain white socks, it was the other main feature of the home strip for years."

CELTIC MATCHWORN

"I regard the team that wore that 1987/88 jersey as 'my' Celtic team. They were my first team of heroes; the team that captured my heart and imagination. It should come as no surprise that the first replica I ever owned was the green and white hoops from the memorable centenary campaign.

"Ever since the centenary year, I was fascinated and drawn to Celtic's hooped jersey and later this prompted me to start buying 1980s Celtic shirts that I had previously owned as a child. After some research on players' jerseys, I learned through collectors that they had some noticeable differences from the replicas I had been buying for several years. This interest would lead me on my journey of collecting match worn jerseys.

"My collection has developed as I have added jerseys from important games throughout Celtic's history, including cup finals, European finals, testimonials and obscure or hard-to-find shirts. I dedicate a lot of effort into researching archive footage and photographs from games in order to identify which jerseys were worn in certain games and by specific players. This process is more problematic for pre-1994 shirts due to there being no numbers on the hoops for domestic games. I now have between 90

and 100 match worn and player-issue Celtic jerseys, with my favourite being the 1980-82 home shirt. This is for no other reason than its sheer beauty and simplicity.

"The Celtic jersey that I'd love to add to my collection would be the first-ever shirt. None are known to be in existence, but there might be one in someone's attic somewhere and they may not even know the relevance of it.

"What do the green and white hoops represent for me? Unity and a togetherness. A bond that holds so many people from different walks of life together as one for 90 minutes."
www.celticmatchworn.co.uk

DANIEL HUGHES

"The green and white of Celtic has always been part of my family. So much so that it is now more of a habit than a hobby. The first season ticket I ever had was free due to me being a Celtic Pools agent. That was 30 years ago and I have been a season-ticket holder ever since.

"A few years ago, I was given Johan Mjällby's match worn top and shorts and that gave me the bug to get started with my own jersey collection. I then started buying shirts on online auction sites, and some of my personal favourites include a lime green European jersey, a Kieran Tierney home shirt that he wore against Aberdeen, and a Charlie Mulgrew black and yellow away top that was worn against Kilmarnock at Rugby Park.

"The early eighties pinstripe jerseys are two that I'd love to get my hands on someday, and I'll keep searching because they don't become available very often. We wore the green with white pinstripes version in the European Cup against Ajax in the Olympic Stadium in 1982. Charlie Nicholas and George McCluskey scored the goals that night to secure a famous European victory."

JAMIE FOX

"It would perhaps sound crass if I started off by saying that Celtic mean everything to me, but they really do.

"Thinking back just over the past 10 years, there is not a day goes by that I am not doing something relating to Celtic. Some 23 years ago, I met my wife Mary at a Celtic event in Bairds Bar in Glasgow's Gallowgate. Ten years later, I proposed to her in the Benidorm Palace at Celtic's first European convention, and a year later we got married in the Riviera Hotel, Las Vegas, at the Lisbon Lions' 40th Anniversary Convention, where my reception included 50 of my family and friends, not to mention the 3,000 Celtic supporters and the Lisbon Lions in attendance at the Friday night Grand Ball.

"As much as I adore the hoops, I always loved it when I went to the game and Celtic ran out wearing all-green, all-white or all-yellow kits. I was also fond of the white strip with green hoops around the collar and cuffs.

"I collect early Celtic items but I am not actually that into collecting match worn jerseys, even though I do have quite a few. The first I obtained was 30 years ago when I acquired John Clark's strip. Twelve years ago, I also purchased a jersey that I would class as the Holy Grail - worn by Billy McNeill against Racing Club of Argentina

in the World Club Championship first leg at Hampden Park on 18th October 1967.

"In order to complete this purchase, I had to send a four-figure sum electronically to a Buenos Aires-based sports management company who were representing former Racing Club captain Oscar Martin. Several Celtic shirt collectors told me it was a huge risk to send so much money electronically to Argentina. A few weeks later, I also bought the match pennant that McNeill swapped with Martin before the match. This cost £32 in postage, but it arrived within three days from Buenos Aires. I never considered the risk involved because at the forefront of my mind was that I was rescuing rare items from Celtic's history from the Argentine. I didn't realise it at the time, but recent research suggests that not even Billy himself had one of his match worn Celtic jerseys. I believe that this is the only one out there, although we might find others in the future that were swapped during Celtic's many European exploits.

"Celtic's green and white hoops represent everything that is good about a club: the green for the colour of the grass we play on; the white for the purity of the football we must play."

ACKNOWLEDGEMENTS

The author would like to thank the following group of people, who helped to make this book possible:

Tom Boyd, for writing the Foreword. Neilly Mochan, for his friendship, wealth of knowledge and unrivalled collection of Celtic jerseys. Tom Campbell, Pat Woods, David Potter, Ian McCallum, Brendan Sweeney and John McLauchlan for their ongoing assistance and encouragement. Andy Murdoch, Simon Weir, Gordon Cowan, Jim Greenan, John Fallon, Barry McLuskie, Simon Shakeshaft and Brian Gilda for their time in helping to fill in some important gaps in the story. Michael Mlotkiewicz, for giving me this idea and supporting me throughout the process. Craig Brown, Neil Spowart, and Kelvin Craig, for taking the photographs. Jim Drewett, Ed Davis, Doug Cheeseman, Toby Trotman, and everyone at Vision Sports Publishing for their patience and belief in the book. Damian Donald, Daniel Hughes, Colm Clancy, Joe Arcari, Paul Lamb, Malcolm McDougall, Jamie Fox, Stuart McDonnell, The Celtic Shirt, and Celtic Matchworn, for allowing me access to their jersey collections. Kerry Keenan, Ian Henderson and Danielle Haughey for assisting us at Celtic Park. John Buckley, the ACSOM team and everyone who tunes into the show for their constant support. Lynsey and Paul for giving me the strength to continue with a project that took seven years to complete.

Paul John Dykes, October 2022